TO

_____

FROM

_____

DATE

_____

100 DAYS OF

Believing Bigger

DEVOTIONAL JOURNAL

MARSHAWN EVANS DANIELS

DaySpring
LIVE YOUR FAITH

100 Days of Believing Bigger: Devotional Journal
Copyright © Marshawn Evans Daniels
First Edition, September 2020

Published by:

21154 Highway 16 East
Siloam Springs, AR 72761
dayspring.com

Written by: Marshawn Evans Daniels
Cover Design by: Jessica Wei

Printed in China
Prime: J2432
ISBN: 978-1-64454-811-0

Hey there, Life Changer,

This I know for sure: every woman longs to be seen, selected, and significant. Isn't it interesting that we long for what we already are? In the eyes of God, we're *already* everything heaven ever wanted and more. But as women, we often don't *feel* that way.

We wrestle with self-doubt, worry, perfectionism, toxic thinking, and surrender. And that's just this morning! Navigating the twists and turns of a faith adventure with God isn't always the picturesque garden stroll depicted. I used to feel a deep disconnect with how we "beautify" the gospel. It creates an impossible standard, leading us to feel as if we have to look and talk the part. If we don't, we feel flawed, broken, and in need of so much work that we couldn't possibly be ready for God to use us right now.

If you've ever felt that way, you're not alone. It is my hope that during our sacred time together, you'll embrace the courage it takes to truly *Believe Bigger* about who you are, why you matter, and what you're here to do *right now* for such a time as this.

Your picking up this devotional journal is not at all an accident. This is a destiny appointment. Odds are, God has been trying to get your attention for some time. And the truth is, you're being recruited to a higher dimension of purpose. God longs to spend quality time with you so that He can awaken something magnificent within you...and so God can simply love on you, too.

You see, it's embracing and bathing in the love of God that leads us into a place of bigger belief, boldness, purpose, and surrender.

I'm honored that our paths have crossed. Each daily devotion revolves around four pillars:

- Scripture—It's important that we anchor our spiritual growth in the Word of God. It's the soil that enables us to grow and multiply;
- Reflection—Each daily lesson is designed to give you a chance to place the Scripture in context and relate it to your personal life;
- Journal Prompts—Guided journaling enables you to immediately engage the Holy Spirit with specific questions; and
- Simple + Bold Prayers—God already knows the desires of our heart, so simple + bold prayers make it easier for us to focus on intention instead of wordiness.

You may see the same Scripture more than once or the same verse in different translations. I believe in quality over quantity. Spiritual growth isn't about memorizing Scripture like words in a dictionary. It's about hearing what heaven has for you. And, for me, sometimes that happens by going deeper into different dimensions of the same verse. I'd also love for each prayer to be like a permission slip, where you affirm a new reality and claim a new dimension for your life in the moment.

My hope is that you'll discover how incredible you really are. There is a warrior on the inside of you, a woman with a big mission and a supernatural message. It's time to step into your next season with focus and faith. It's time to *Believe Bigger*.

Let's do this.

marshawn

Trust Made Simple

Jesus replied,
"You do not realize now what I am doing,
but later you will understand."
—JOHN 13:7 NIV

G od is more concerned with our trust than our talent...more committed to our character than our career...and more interested in obedience than sacrifice. Because of our desire to get what we want when we want it, though, we naturally tend to rush the process and attempt to put God on our time line. We set our expectations high, create our own schedule, and start racing toward that finish line. Then, when our expectations aren't met, we feel frustrated because we haven't met our goals. But there is something God wants more than your speed, hard work, or mighty efforts. God wants your *TRUST*—(T)otal (R)eliance (U)pon (S)piritual (T)iming. Not easy, right? Instead, we want to orchestrate. We want to direct. We want to control. And we want answers! However, the truth is that we simply don't know what's best for us. We certainly don't have heaven's elevated view. And if we're acting in haste, we can get in the way of God's intended blessings for us. Trusting God is trusting His timing and believing that you can rely upon Him in both the wait and the pursuit. God is never late. He is always on time.

How has trusting God's timing been a struggle for you? What might God be trying to teach you in the process?

_____

_____

_____

_____

_____

_____

_____

_____

_____

_____

_____

_____

_____

_____

_____

_____

_____

PRAY

Lord, thank You for being more concerned with my being than with my doing. Equip me with an unshakable level of trust in You and Your timing. You are perfect in every way.

AMEN.

Seeing the Unseen

Faith led Noah to listen when God warned him
about the things in the future that he could not see.
He obeyed God and built a ship to save his family.
Through faith Noah condemned the world
and received God's approval that comes through faith.
—HEBREWS 11:7 GW

Noah's story is a wonderful example of what it looks like to truly TRUST God. Think about it—Noah was obedient, patient, and willing to be seen as "crazy" by others who didn't understand what He was doing. They couldn't see what He saw or hear what He heard. Remember, trust is what enables us to access the voice of God with greater intensity and clarity. These qualities protected Noah and preserved his legacy and family. He trusted God's instruction even when others humiliated him. He took the time to build the ark and didn't rush. After the flood, Noah first sent a raven and then a dove to test the land to see if it was ready for his family to emerge. When the dove returned without a branch, Noah knew that the place for his "feet" was not yet ready—water still covered the land. But later the dove returned with a branch, signaling that the wait was over. Building our spiritual trust is the primary way God equips us to experience the incredible.

What would have become of Noah and his family if he'd ignored the message (i.e., the lack of a branch) and instead decided that it was the right time to step out?

_____

_____

_____

_____

_____

_____

_____

_____

_____

_____

_____

_____

_____

PRAY

Lord, Your ways are perfect, and Your timing is pristine.
Create in me a desire to see in the realm of the unseen.
And equip me to trust and act upon Your instruction
regardless of opinion or conditions.

AMEN.

Perfect Timing

*Trust in the LORD with all your heart and
lean not on your own understanding;
in all your ways submit to Him,
and He will make your paths straight.*
—PROVERBS 3:5–6 NIV

When it comes to *TRUST*, remember, we're talking about Total Reliance Upon Spiritual Timing...not just partial trust in the areas where we feel the odds are in our favor. We must become intentional when it comes to no longer trusting the wrong things like yourself, your experience, your intellect...You may be good, but God is great. God's got a higher, wider, and more eternal view. This is a special time to trust God with your whole heart, especially the parts you've been holding back out of fear of fully letting go. Disbelief disrupts our destiny. We block miracles when we give God just a small piece versus all of us. It can seem scary. And that's okay. God isn't afraid of or turned off by your emotions or feelings. Instead, He wants you to bring those cares and worries to Him. Even in the midst of frustration, know that every detour and delay has been divinely orchestrated. Remember, God knows the ideal timing for you to arrive at your destination.

Day 3

Tell me, where are YOU struggling with trusting God's timing? What lesson do you think God is trying to teach you about patience, spiritual intimacy, and preparation? Where do you get stuck?

_____

_____

_____

_____

_____

_____

_____

_____

_____

_____

_____

_____

_____

_____

_____

PRAY

God, You are the One who created time. You are in control. You're never behind, and I thank You that I am always exactly where I need to be to trust in, listen to, and follow You.

AMEN.

Releasing Perfectionism

The Lord will perfect that which concerns me;
Your mercy, O Lord, endures forever;
do not forsake the works of Your hands.
—PSALM 138:8 NKJV

It's easy for us to trust in our own abilities, accomplishments, and experiences as indications of our capabilities. The good news is that as a daughter created in the image of the Most High God, you are indeed full of infinite potential and possibility. But even as a carrier of God's divine DNA, we're still limited by the human body, mind, and perspective. God alone has the entire world in His hands; He has the only view that sees all things interwoven from beginning to the end. And the even *greater* news is that God is far better at working out all things for you than you are. Above, the word "perfect" is used as an action word. It means to refine, improve, and put on the finishing touches. Perfectionism, our wanting to control circumstances to create favorable outcomes, can be dangerous to our destiny. You see, your destiny isn't really yours. You're a critical part of God's bigger plan, but let's not forget that it's *His* plan we must learn to joyously and expectantly surrender to. Know that He will perfect everything that concerns you. Perfecting is what God loves to do.

Day 4

Have you been worried about how something is going to work out? How does worry lead you to meddle and make things happen as opposed to trusting God to work things out?

_____

_____

_____

_____

_____

_____

_____

_____

_____

_____

_____

_____

_____

_____

_____

_____

PRAY

Lord, Your ways are marvelous and soaked in significance.
When Your hands touch my life, failure is impossible. Thank You
for replacing my perfectionism with Your perfect will and way.

AMEN.

Water Walking

Jesus: Indeed, come.
—MATTHEW 14:29 THE VOICE

The disciples traveled quite a bit with Jesus by boat. They spent every day with him, but for some reason, on this occasion they couldn't recognize Jesus walking toward them on the water. They weren't comforted or even amazed by a miracle unfolding before their very eyes. No, the Scripture says that they were so terrified, they thought Jesus was a ghost. How interesting that we can confuse what is actually help as something that appears to be harmful. When Jesus told them, "Be still. It is I. You have nothing to fear," His disciple Peter was the only one who was drawn toward the mystery. Peter said, "Lord, if it is really You, then command me to meet You on the water." When Jesus said, "Indeed, come," Peter stepped out onto the water and began to walk toward Jesus. But when he realized how high the waves were, he became frightened and started to sink (v. 27–30). I love that Peter was brave, that he asked to be part of an impossible miracle with Jesus. What trust! But Peter is no different than you and me. When we look at our circumstances, aka the waves, our faith is punctured. It's not the waves that cause us to sink—it's putting our trust in our circumstances. As Jesus says in verse 31, "Why did you doubt…?"

Which circumstances in your life are like the waves that intimidated Peter? How might Jesus be using these waves to show you how to walk on water?

_____

_____

_____

_____

_____

_____

_____

_____

_____

_____

_____

_____

_____

_____

_____

_____

_____

PRAY

Lord, make me like Peter. Draw me out of the boat
of the familiar and safe man-made methods. I commit to keep
my eyes on You. Invite me into miracles, signs, and wonders.

AMEN.

The Faithfulness of God

He who calls you is faithful; he will surely do it.
—I THESSALONIANS 5:24 ESV

For doers and achievers, it can be difficult to be still and wait to see how God's plan is going to unfold. It's natural for us to want to know what's ahead and how it's all going to come together and when. Maybe you're the type who's not afraid to do her part. Give you a goal, and you'll make it happen. But what if your part is letting go? Sure, it's easier said than done—but this season is more about surrender than anything else. And, surrender is a complicated balance when we're trying to help our families, build a dream, and change lives in the process! Your efforts won't always be "enough" to create the outcomes you desire. Here's the good news, though. The verse above gifts us with a stress-alleviating promise: God will surely do it. Not you. Not me. *He.* There are some breakthroughs that can only transpire with the move of God's hand. We can't force it; we can only flow in it.

How are you getting in the way of what God is doing by trying to make something happen versus putting it in His hands?

_____

_____

_____

_____

_____

_____

_____

_____

_____

_____

_____

_____

_____

_____

_____

_____

_____

PRAY

Lord, my hands naturally default to busyness. Remove the spirit of anxiousness from my heart so that I can rest in Your timing. Align the work of my hands with Your heart and plan.

AMEN.

Undeniable Consistency

Jesus Christ is the same
yesterday and today and forever.
—HEBREWS 13:8 ESV

I remember when I was a single woman dating and desiring to be married. Dating can be incredibly enlightening. It gives an opportunity to see someone's character, integrity, and personality. But most importantly, it is a chance to evaluate a person's consistency. If someone isn't consistent in your life, they aren't really worthy of your trust. That goes for any relationship in your life. The reality of humanity is that people will disappoint you—and you will disappoint others, even if you don't intend any harm. We're flawed and imperfect, but Jesus is not. There is no one more selfless, more giving, more attentive, and more interested in your life. His love is perfect, wholly pure, and designed to passionately pursue you every day and in every way. We must be careful not to misconstrue the inherent mystery of God as inconsistency. His love and intention are unchanging. Our intimacy with Him reveals His consistency toward us. Plus, miracles spring up from the soil of supernatural mystery. The unknown makes way for the unbelievable.

How has disappointment in others put a dent in your trust when it comes to your relationship with God?

_____

_____

_____

_____

_____

_____

_____

_____

_____

_____

_____

_____

_____

_____

PRAY

Lord, forgive me for viewing You through a faulty lens.
Help me to permanently release the frustration
of past letdowns from others. Teach me to trust You
no matter what others say or do.

AMEN.

Secret Things

There is a God in heaven who reveals mysteries.
—DANIEL 2:28 NIV

Secret things. Revealing 'em is the specialty of the Holy Spirit. It's a whisper filled with wisdom. It often feels untimely and inconvenient, but that's how heaven works. And it's how God's promises come to fruition. You see, a major life shift often happens with a gentle nudge. We can miss it when we're operating from a place of fatigue, worry, or doubt. However, trust changes *what* we see and *how* we hear. It takes open eyes to see and ready ears to hear a destiny tug, inviting us into the very thing we've been praying for. Listening for those divine tugs and recognizing that they are not just coincidences will be your secret weapon when it comes to entering the next level of what God has for you. It's those whispers that accelerate His vision and propel you into your promised land. And it's those whispers from God that reveal God's unique path and unconventional plan for your life. We cannot seize what we don't believe. Trusting God is the key to perceiving what God is doing.

What whispers from God have you been doubting, overanalyzing, second-guessing or flat-out ignoring?

_____

_____

_____

_____

_____

_____

_____

_____

_____

_____

_____

_____

_____

_____

_____

_____

PRAY

Lord, You are always speaking, leading, and guiding.
Thank You for removing the mental clutter that blocks me
from trusting Your whisper. May I trust You in the midst of
uncertainty and also appreciate the beauty of Your mystery.

AMEN.

Knowing God Hears You

This is the confidence we have in approaching God:
that if we ask anything according to His will, He hears us.
—I JOHN 5:14 NIV

Faith is having a steadfast belief in something (or someone) without having proof. It's hopeful, optimistic, and looks toward the future with possibility and expectancy. Trust is similar, but it is more about actively relying upon someone's character and consistency. When we operate within trust, we're able to take action based on that person's integrity and reliability. For that reason, trust is harder than faith. We can believe that God is capable of all things, but it's another thing to fully entrust God with every area of our lives. By entrust, I mean to act *as if* God has already worked things out versus questioning *whether* He'll come through. So the question becomes, do you have faith in our God being capable and able but struggle to trust whether God is willing and ready? If so, you're not alone! Each day, God is seeking to strengthen our entire belief system and teaching us to align with His heart. That doesn't mean that God will necessarily answer in the ways that we want. That's neither faith nor trust. However, as the verse above reminds us, when we come to God in a posture of surrender, we can trust that He is listening and hears every single word.

How much peace does it give you to know that God actually hears you?

Lord, I am humbled and encouraged that You are wholeheartedly interested in every facet of my life. Thank You for hearing me. Keep me in alignment with Your Holy Spirit.
AMEN.

Remembering Eternity

And we know that for those who love God
all things work together for good,
for those who are called according to his purpose.
—ROMANS 8:28 ESV

Life doesn't always make sense. It's natural to anxiously wonder whether it's all going to work out. Faith says that we believe God to be bigger than our circumstances and that He can do anything and everything. But God isn't a performer waiting to fulfill the latest desires of our heart. Yes, God is the Provider. He is *also* Father. The core of our relationship with God, and God's relationship with us, is love. Love is like a portal that invites us into the protective covering and supernatural plan of God. It's so easy to forget that we're part of something bigger than what we know. God sees every moment and strategically interweaves our moments, joys, and frustrations into the lives of others. He doesn't do this *for* us—to please us or satisfy us. He does this for the *master* purpose: eternity. Our trust in God must first be based upon a firm reliance in His undeniable love for us—to never abandon us. And then we must trust that what's happening in our lives is actually working together for a good that is eternal and magnificent.

What's happening in your life is connected to a bigger plan orchestrated by God. How can this truth help you reframe your current circumstances and build more trust in what God is doing?

_____

_____

_____

_____

_____

_____

_____

_____

_____

_____

_____

_____

_____

PRAY

Lord, I don't always understand what You're up to,
but You are worthy of my trust and surrender. Thank You
for choosing me to be an instrument of Your holy agenda.
What a joy to be included in Your eternal plan!

AMEN.

The Purpose Pathway: Workmanship (PART 1)

*For we are Christ's **workmanship**,*
created in Christ Jesus, to do good works,
which He prepared in advance for us to do.
—EPHESIANS 2:10

This is one of my favorite Scriptures, because inside it lies four keys to discovering one's divine purpose. Take a look at the words themselves: "workmanship," "good works," "advance," and "do." "Workmanship" means that you are a custom creation, that there is no one like you. Nobody else has the stuff you have or has been designed the way that you were created. You are a tailor-made, one-of-a-kind masterpiece. Because of that, we should never try to imitate or replicate what's already been done. No one has your God-given fingerprint. And God doesn't repeat Himself. He made you because you are a unique expression of His DNA with a specific mission that literally cannot be fulfilled by anyone else. The world needs what you have—your mind, gifts, and personality. Part of the purpose discovery process is embracing that you matter and were specifically handcrafted by heaven for such a time as this.

Do you embrace your own uniqueness? In what ways do you struggle to believe in your relevancy and magnificence?

_____

_____

_____

_____

_____

_____

_____

_____

_____

_____

_____

_____

_____

_____

_____

_____

_____

_____

_____

PRAY

Lord, give me eyes to see me the way You see me.
I am Your custom craftsmanship. Thank You
for making me unique, magnetic, and necessary.
Help me to own my significance and magnificence.
AMEN.

The Purpose Pathway:
Good Works (PART 2)

For we are Christ's workmanship,
*created in Christ Jesus, to do **good works**,*
which He prepared in advance for us to do.
—EPHESIANS 2:10

As we continue to break down the four key parts in the Scripture above (workmanship, good works, advance, and do), remember that we're delving into the topic of purpose. Each word is a purpose clue. The next part is the phrase "good works." So often we miss the pathway into a higher purpose because we're either looking for something impressive (worthy of praise) or something perfect. We don't want to be a disappointment to God, and we don't want to get it wrong. Here's the thing: being able to figure out exactly what God wants you to do, where, when, and how, is really an impossible standard. So let's take the pressure off *clarity* and shift into something better, which is *courage*. The passage above is filled with permission. You're *already* created to do good works. Just start there. Start with something—anything—that will help people. Eventually you'll find patterns and clues to guide you into a more focused direction. Whenever you operate with the mission of helping others, know that heaven is with you, covering you, and opening more doors for you.

How do you want to help people? What is something simple you can commit to do today?

_____

_____

_____

_____

_____

_____

_____

_____

_____

_____

_____

_____

_____

PRAY

*Lord, thank You for reminding me that everything You do
has unlimited purpose. Any moment You are present
is an incredible gift. Fill me with Your heart and mind.
Guide my choices, make me a light, and remind me
that good works are in my spiritual DNA.*

AMEN.

The Purpose Pathway: In Advance (PART 3)

For we are Christ's workmanship,
created in Christ Jesus, to do good works,
which He prepared __in advance__ for us to do.
—EPHESIANS 2:10

Purpose is such a powerful force. Discovering one's purpose is more about realignment than it is about achievement or attainment of something new. In the last two entries, we explored the purpose clues found in the phrases "workmanship" and "good works" from the passage above. Our next purpose clue is "in advance." So often we're looking outside ourselves for clues about who we're *supposed* to be or who we *could* be. This is a flawed start to purpose discovery. We are *Christ's* workmanship, created in *His* image and for *His* purpose. Our identity is found in our premade design. It's not about passion—what we choose to do. It's about permission—surrendering to what we were born to do. You've already been prepared *in advance* for destiny. You have everything you need. Sure, we all need refinement and stewardship, but God's unique blueprint for your life was predeposited in you before you were born, and when we allow Christ into our lives, that decision supernaturally activates it.

Take a moment and think about how you've always enjoyed helping others. It doesn't have to be a major event. What stirs your heart? What everyday impact do you want to have on others? How has God prebuilt you to elevate others?

_____

_____

_____

_____

_____

_____

_____

_____

_____

_____

_____

PRAY

Lord, I'm so grateful that nothing in my life takes You by surprise. Thank You for equipping me in advance to be a catalyst for impact. Give me Your eyes to see the specific qualities and gifts You've already given me to fulfill my life's mission. I'm ready.

AMEN.

The Purpose Pathway:

Do (PART 4)

For we are Christ's workmanship,
created in Christ Jesus, to do good works,
which He prepared in advance for us to __do__.
—EPHESIANS 2:10

We've looked at the first three purpose clues found in the phrases "workmanship," "good works," and "in advance." The final purpose clue from this Scripture is the word "do." Just as a tire isn't made for the purpose of sitting on a shelf, you're not here to sit on the sidelines of life either. Everything God designs and births has an intentional purpose and a specific assignment that grows and expands over time. Purpose is not an intellectual exercise; it's a contact sport. We're supposed to engage with uncertainty, fear, and challenges. That's where we find out what God has predeposited inside of us. And what a spectacular discovery it is! But first it will be intimidating. Stepping into a bigger vision for your life is supposed to be daunting. That's because your calling and vision are bigger than you, which is also why you need God's guidance and grace to see them through. God can't bless actions we never take.

What is something you can do to have a greater impact on others right now?
Be specific. What fears do you have? How are your fears a distraction?

_____

_____

_____

_____

_____

_____

_____

_____

_____

_____

_____

_____

_____

PRAY

Lord, help me to realize and remember that I'm already
more than enough to impact where I am right now.
Order my footsteps as I recall that I am prebuilt
to do good works every day and in every way.

AMEN.

Your Born Identity

*I pray that the eyes of your heart
may be enlightened in order that you may know
the hope to which He has called you....*
—EPHESIANS 1:18 NIV

Purpose is not just a fancy way of finding your passion. It's the process of entering God's plan.

It's about discovering your divine assignment and fulfilling your God-given life mission. Here's the thing: stepping into what God has for you will *always* require you to believe bigger. You see, to believe bigger means to believe beyond who you think you are. It requires you to be willing to see yourself as necessary, incredibly gifted, and limitlessly impactful. God neither consults your past nor your résumé when He maps out your future. And He isn't confined to your passions either. Those are the things you've learned to do— your *formed* identity. But in order to enter a new level of impact and meaning, you must be willing to embrace your true *born* identity. *How* you see yourself will determine *what* you see for yourself.

How is your past—the ups and downs—possibly blocking you from believing in your untapped potential?

_____

_____

_____

_____

_____

_____

_____

_____

_____

_____

_____

_____

_____

PRAY

Lord, give me Your eyes to see myself the way You see me.
Help me to grasp both the magnitude and the simplicity
of Your higher calling and purpose for my life. And give me
the courage to believe in what You have for me.

AMEN.

Leaving Your Comfort Zone

And those He predestined, He also called;
those He called, He also justified;
those He justified, He also glorified.
—ROMANS 8:30 NIV

Purpose is not supposed to be an ever-seeking, never-finding, illusive, impossible-to-grasp type of thing. God wants you to understand your purpose. Everything you've encountered—even the awful things—have been part of your journey. It's easy to feel as if our imperfections disqualify us from being used by God in a mighty way, but let's not forget that Jesus hand-selected everyday people to be His disciples. His mother Mary was incredibly young and must have felt unqualified for a task as massive as raising the Messiah. And then there was John the Baptist, who lived like a hippie in the woods but was the only one heaven anointed to baptize others and make a way for Jesus. God doesn't use the same faulty, fickle standards of the world. He's not looking for your accomplishments; He's looking for your *availability*. However, entering a higher level of purpose with God will require a radical mind shift. The inner beliefs that got you where you are won't get you into your promised land. It's time to leave your comfort zone to access your glory zone.

Where do you feel God leading you next? How is insecurity or feeling unqualified getting in the way of you accepting your calling?

_____

_____

_____

_____

_____

_____

_____

_____

_____

_____

_____

_____

_____

_____

_____

_____

_____

_____

_____

PRAY

Lord, help me to be kind to myself and to find joy and purpose in my imperfections. You've recruited me because I'm worthy. Mature me, focus me, and equip me with the mindset needed to bring You glory.

AMEN.

Believing in Your Gifts

For God's gifts and His call are irrevocable.
—ROMANS 11:29 NIV

Your purpose isn't lost. Purpose isn't even something you find. It's something you uncover. God previously designed you for it, and you're already being guided by it. There are hidden patterns embedded in your experiences containing God's direction and ultimate intention for your life. And God has preloaded you with special gifts, insights, and abilities, along with a unique personality, that actually reveals His game plan. When *we* look at our lives, we see chaos. When *God* looks at our lives, He sees a map and a masterpiece. He sees your beginning and your end, and all of heaven (even right now) is constantly seeking to move you forward and closer to your divine destination. God is a God of impeccable order, intention, and structure. Nothing that has occurred in your life is a coincidence, and you're not behind. The good news is that your calling and giftings never expire. When you fully believe in your gifts, that's when miracles start happening through you. The path heaven desires for you is found in how God designed you.

What do you feel are your gifts? How might they be tied to your purpose or calling?

_____

_____

_____

_____

_____

_____

_____

_____

_____

_____

_____

_____

_____

_____

PRAY

Lord, thank You for prewiring me with Your DNA and everything
I need to be an effective ambassador and extension of You.
Show me my gifts; groom me in the areas where I need to grow;
and lead me directly to those You want me to serve.

AMEN.

Authorized to Impact

They were completely amazed at His teaching;
because He was teaching them as one having
[God-given] authority, and not as the scribes.
—MARK 1:22 AMP

As young girls, we slowly but steadily internalize some faulty thinking and become wired to reach for what we think is appropriate (the right thing to do) or attainable (the best we can do). When we are fed protocol instead of purpose, we settle for less. Jesus shows us what it looks like, however, to trade *protocol* living for *permission* living. He didn't have traditional religious titles, degrees, or positions that would have qualified Him, by social standards, to teach about heaven, much less perform miracles anytime and anyplace. He was young, just entering His thirties...but He was anointed by God with a fresh message that the world didn't even know it needed. God is saying the same thing about you. It's fine to get traditional training, and it's important to be an intelligent, responsible steward of your talents. The problem is when protocol—how things are supposed to go—becomes an idol. Nothing about God is predictable. The Holy Spirit is uncontainable. Your authority doesn't come from man, paved paths, and predictable plans; it comes from the King of kings.

Have you been waiting for someone to approve how you do what you believe God is calling you to? What would it look like to give yourself permission to pursue that calling regardless of qualification or custom?

_____

_____

_____

_____

_____

_____

_____

_____

_____

_____

_____

_____

_____

_____

_____

_____

PRAY

Lord, You are my commander in chief. Your will is my desire, and Your Word is my direction. Help me to detox from protocol, outdated beliefs, old conventions, and anything that would block me from being who You've built me to be.

AMEN.

Cultivate Your Curiosity

There the angel of the Lord appeared to him
in flames of fire from within a bush.
Moses saw that though the bush was on fire
it did not burn up. So Moses thought, "I will go over and
see this strange sight—why the bush does not burn up."
—EXODUS 3:2–3 NIV

I'm convinced that the enemy plots with the spirit of the ordinary to get us to settle...to have us stay where we are...to remain content and silence our calling when it knocks. If the enemy can get a woman to fear or, better yet, to ignore the holy whisper that calls her onto the battlefield of purpose and significance, then she'll never even know she's living beneath her birthright. Although he's a man, Moses is probably one of my favorite examples of this. He was an outcast, a foreigner, and an orphan abandoned by his mother. He was tending to the fields, going through the motions and doing the ordinary, when God disrupted Moses's life in a radical way. A burning bush—that must have been a sight to see! Most people would have run the other way, but something inside Moses prompted him to walk *toward* the fire. He was able to discern the moment as a holy encounter...something new calling him. I believe it was the spirit of curiosity dwelling within him. Curiosity, a desire to know more about what God has for you, is the secret to shifting into a higher purpose. Curiosity is always the catalyst to calling. And it's the antidote to the spirit of the ordinary. The voice of heaven is leading you off the mundane path of predictability and onto a more anointed, adventurous one.

What is a current example of a "burning bush" in your life? What are you curious to discover about yourself and what God might be revealing about your future?

_____

_____

_____

_____

_____

_____

_____

_____

_____

_____

_____

_____

_____

_____

_____

PRAY

Lord, You've made me in Your image, which means that I am a warrior. Let me run toward the burning bush, as I long to hear directly from You and to encounter You. I'm ready.

AMEN.

Own Your Vision

Then the LORD replied:
"Write down the revelation and make it plain on tablets
so that a herald may run with it."
—HABAKKUK 2:2 NIV

God speaks to us in such unique and intimate ways. He can get your attention by any means necessary, but the real question is whether you're paying attention. When God seeks to shift you, He almost always begins by stirring your heart and agitating your comfort. The next thing He'll do is give you a glimpse of where He is taking you next. Most of us ignore the signs, tugs, and recurring messages. We say we want to be used by God, but then we avoid all situations disrupting the predictability that makes us feel safe and secure. But to believe bigger is to ask God for a bigger vision *and* to believe that you're worthy of more. Sometimes we confuse the desire to experience more with being greedy and discontent. Balance is important, but desire is also divine. Ecclesiastes 1:7 says, "All streams flow into the sea, yet the sea is never full." You want more because God designed you for more in His limitless image. He won't force you into it. God gives a bigger vision to those ready to make bigger decisions.

What's the big vision you have for your life? Embrace the fact that God wants you to dream without limits. Write down your vision—what you desire to experience, who you want to impact, and how you want to glorify God.

_____

_____

_____

_____

_____

_____

_____

_____

_____

_____

_____

_____

_____

_____

_____

_____

_____

PRAY

Lord, there are no limits in heaven. Since heaven lives within me, take the limits off my life, my mind, and my eyes. Show me new places and prepare me for new provisions as I embrace Your bigger mission and vision.

AMEN.

Embracing You

*Let's just go ahead and be what we were made to be,
without enviously or pridefully comparing ourselves
with each other, or trying to be something we aren't.*
—ROMANS 12:6–7 THE MESSAGE

In a world filled with protocol, a never-ending list of dos and don'ts, and the pressure to be perfect, it can seem impossible to discover who you really are and what you're here to be and do. I've always loved how the Scripture above gives us a direct glimpse into God's game plan: *be what you were made to be*. This is at the heart of divine reinvention—coming into alignment with our true assignment. The way God uniquely made you is a clue as to what He wants you to do. Nothing about you is a mistake. This verse is also a reminder of the permission you've *already* received to be uniquely you as a daughter of the Most High. Plus, God won't bless who you pretend to be. So let's stop conforming, shrinking, dimming your light, and running from who and what you were always meant to be, say, create, and do. We're waiting on you...the real you. And that's the version of you heaven needs too.

How have you been chipping away at who you are by trying to be what everyone else needs? What is God now showing you about yourself that needs to come out of hiding?

_____

_____

_____

_____

_____

_____

_____

_____

_____

_____

_____

_____

_____

_____

PRAY

Lord, help me to trust the unique way You've formed and fashioned my personality, my thoughts, my perspective, my voice, and my abilities. I release any thoughts of inferiority and embrace how You've designed me beautifully and strategically.

AMEN.

You Are Capable

I can do all this through Christ
who gives me strength.
—PHILIPPIANS 4:13

Our trust in God is not somehow separate from our belief in ourselves. To the contrary, divine trust and self-belief are linked together by the umbilical cord of purpose. We cannot fulfill our destiny merely with one or the other; we need both. We need a healthy and hearty self-image to even have the audacity to pursue all God has in store for us. Notice that I didn't say we need a strong self-image to believe in God. I meet women (and men) every day who love God but don't really like themselves. The truth be told, most of us women spend an inordinate amount of time trying to "fix" our faults or find a way to simply "live with" ourselves. Well. I've discovered this: if you don't learn to *celebrate* yourself, you'll settle for a life where you simply *tolerate* yourself. That's not God's vision for you—you are His daughter. You are His custom creation, and He desires that you love who you are and grow to operate with supernatural courage using the gifts, personality, and intellect He gave you.

How has self-doubt been holding you back? What is the new story God is inviting you to write when it comes to your view of yourself?

PRAY

*Lord, help me to shed all the negative beliefs
and faulty thoughts about myself. I declare that I am
who You say I am, regardless of what anyone else
says or thinks and regardless of my past.
I am capable. I am wonderful. I am chosen.
In Jesus's name,* AMEN.

You Are a Vessel

That is why, for Christ's sake,
I delight in weaknesses, in insults, in hardships,
in persecutions, in difficulties.
For when I am weak, then I am strong.
—II CORINTHIANS 12:10 NIV

What if what *we see* as personal weaknesses were actually advantages? Society leads us to believe that perfection is what makes us worthy, but that's a lie! Imperfection gives us the opportunity to grow and be made more and more like Christ. We also learn the power of supernatural reliance—us relying on God to do what *only* God can do, through us. For that reason, the verse says, "For when I am weak, then I am strong." As God renews us and meets us when we're down, He has an open window to come in and supply our soul with healing and wisdom, helping us to get back up and show others how to rise and move forward as well. Enduring these growth zones is precisely what advances us into the glory zone. Our strengths are indeed clues as to where God wants us to serve, work, impact, lead, and prosper. Your strengths elevate and improve someone else's life in an area where they may not be as seasoned or skilled as you. And vice versa. God designed it that way so we would be interconnected. Plus, if all were perfect, God would have nothing to perfect. We'd never be able to experience His strength. God's muscle is far better than man power.

Where and when have you felt like you're not good enough or already enough?

_____
_____
_____
_____
_____
_____
_____
_____
_____
_____
_____
_____
_____
_____
_____
_____

PRAY

*Lord, You are the Source of my strength and the force that
enables me to grow. Because of You, nothing is lacking in me.
I am a work in progress and yet, at the same time,
still more than enough. Steer me and strengthen me
into all You've envisioned me to be.*

AMEN.

You Are Incomparable

I praise You because I am
fearfully and wonderfully made;
Your works are wonderful,
I know that full well.
—PSALM 139:14 NIV

As hard as it may be to believe, what God is doing in the lives of others has absolutely nothing to do with what He is seeking to do in you! When we obsess about what others are doing, we make room for doubt to creep in: *You're not doing enough. You're behind. It's too late. You're not as talented. Your life isn't as pretty. You don't have enough.* You just aren't enough. Much of our insecurity comes from our addiction to comparison and trying to keep up to what others seem to be doing and accomplishing. We become mirage-chasers addicted to photoshopped illusions and harvesters of ego, greed, and envy. We think that superficial grass is greener, but it's not. It's still just grass. You are incomparable. There is no one like you. If we spent as much time focusing on our bigger dreams as we do in watching others live theirs, we'd be happier and making a bigger dent in the kingdom. So let us stop comparing and staring. Plus, staring…it's not polite! Comparison cripples our confidence and compromises our calling.

How has comparison hijacked your courage, clarity, and confidence?

PRAY

Lord, give me eyes to see, seize, and savor the wonderfulness You're doing in my life. Remove all envy. Give me the type of focus and discipline that invites Your next-level provision and direction. Make me a faith leaper, not a looker.

AMEN.

You Are Voice

By the word of the LORD the heavens were made,
and all the host of them by the breath of His mouth.
—PSALM 33:6 NKJV

Part of understanding your divine identity is understanding who God is and how you're made in His image. We don't know what God physically looks like, but we do know what He sounds like. Think about how this all started: God spoke and said, "'Let there be light'; and there was light" (Genesis 1:3 NKJV). God is Father. God is Teacher. But I think we often forget how God is first and foremost *Creator*. Not a magician that snapped his fingers and said "Give me some humans." He spoke life into being and, from His words alone, created something out of nothing. Plus, John 1:1 reminds us that "in the beginning was the Word, and the Word was with God, and the Word *was* God" (NIV, emphasis mine). It's who God is. We're created in His image—a living Word. God is voice and uses voice to create new ideas, miracles, and solutions. His voice is both the vision and the vehicle to our promised land. Again we're created in His image here too. When we use our voice as an extension of God's voice, we create the way God creates. To that end, you don't just have *a* voice, you *are* voice. It's central to your identity. Your voice is the larger message that your life and beliefs are naturally meant to convey. Your voice unlocks the greater purpose and possibility in others.

What thoughts come up for you when you begin to embrace the notion that voice is central to your core identity?

_____

_____

_____

_____

_____

_____

_____

_____

_____

_____

_____

_____

_____

_____

_____

_____

PRAY

Lord, thank You for making me in Your image and gifting me with the power to speak life. I long to create as an extension of Your hands and heart. Guide my words. Show me how to declare the message and mission of my life fearlessly.

AMEN.

You Are a Message

Now I want you to know, brothers and sisters,
that what has happened to me has actually served
to advance the gospel.
—PHILIPPIANS 1:12 NIV

Remember, your voice is your greatest supernatural endowment. You are the carrier of a unique message from heaven that only your life experiences and abilities can convey. No one else has lived your life, muddled through your messes, and made it to this moment the way you have. Your story is a one-of-a-kind key that unlocks possibility in others. And that's why our ultimate life's mission is about improving the lives of others by teaching what we've learned along the way. This is purpose made simple, my friend. Our voice connects others with what God needs them to know, hear, and believe. We're His vessels. God's larger vision and pathway for others are revealed when we use our voice. This is why God is calling you higher. Not because of your strengths but because of your story—and, most likely, because of your struggles. Your struggles are connected to your calling and are, in part, what qualify you for greater impact. Others will learn to overcome, conquer, and find their path forward by hearing the word of your testimony.

What past struggles are actually part of a larger message that God is crafting in your life to accomplish a larger mission?

PRAY

Lord, thank You for wasting nothing. Even in the midst of obstacles, You equip me with greater wisdom, vulnerability, and patience. Mold the story of my life however You see fit. I long to manifest Your glory and lead others to You.

AMEN.

You Are Distinctive

For we are the product of His hand,
heaven's poetry etched on lives,
created in the Anointed, Jesus, to accomplish
the good works God arranged long ago.
—EPHESIANS 2:10 THE VOICE

Purpose is *why* God needs you and *how* God made you. Calling is *where* God is sending you. So the true essence of "purpose" is more *personality-oriented* (how God made you), whereas "calling" is more a path and place of assignment. You are the way you are for a reason. I know the little voice in your head keeps whispering that something is wrong with you…that you're too flawed, quirky, broken, and in need of repair or more development, but that's simply not true. God is ready to use you and your personality right where you are right now. What you think of as a mess, God sees as a message and a miracle already in motion. There are things about your life, personality, presence, character, interests, insights, and abilities that are meant to make things work and flow properly and smoothly for others. Our purpose naturally, almost effortlessly, flows from us. Purpose is natural not forced. The way you think, show up, impact, perceive, desire, and serve is all strategic. Becoming who God made you isn't about *discovering* who you are; it's about *becoming more aware* of how you're naturally designed. It's time to harness the attributes that make you *you*—and then embrace them as assets instead of liabilities.

How is your personality a clue to what God designed you to do?

_____

_____

_____

_____

_____

_____

_____

_____

_____

_____

_____

_____

_____

_____

_____

_____

_____

_____

PRAY

Lord, I thank You for making me distinctive by design.
Remove any stubbornness, foulness, and "superficialness"
that would block the best of me from shining and
leading in alignment with Your assignment.

AMEN.

You Are a Leader

"You did not choose Me, but I chose you and appointed you that you should go and bear fruit, and that your fruit should remain, that whatever you ask the Father in My name He may give you."
—JOHN 15:16 NKJV

As women, we have an up-and-down roller coaster–like relationship with the word "leadership." On one hand, we're supposed to be submissive and supportive. We learn much about surrender but less about stepping up. We want to expand the kingdom, but we don't want to step out of place. We want to be a good wife, a pleasing daughter, and a wonderful mother, but we're afraid to admit that our hearts crave something more. And therein lies a holy tension. God desires that we absorb the wisdom of others but also that we never place the perspective of others (and the protocol of the world) above His voice and plan. The ancient truth is that leadership is your birthright. It's in your DNA. God is not a respecter of persons (see Acts 10:34). That means He doesn't intend for just some of his daughters to lead. He designed you for a specific purpose, mission, and assignment. It's not about notoriety, status, titles, or how many people know your name. Leadership is about understanding how God has uniquely wired you to make His name known. Supernatural leadership happens when you use your gifts, voice, and presence to be a representation of God's love, goodness, limitless creativity, hope, and freedom. You have been personally and strategically handcrafted by the Most High God to lead others into His presence, possibility, and eternity. Don't be scared to shift, ashamed to bear abundant fruit, nor shy about asking God for provision. There is nothing holy about hiding. You were born to lead, built to move others forward, and chosen to rise up for such a time as this.

Where are you feeling led to lead next?

_____
_____
_____
_____
_____
_____
_____
_____
_____
_____
_____
_____
_____
_____
_____
_____
_____

PRAY

Lord, You have been gracious with Your attention and intention for me. Anchor me in the anointing of leadership. Reveal my assignment and equip me to serve passionately and proficiently.

AMEN.

You Are a Warrior

*The weapons we fight with
are not the weapons of the world.
On the contrary, they have divine power
to demolish strongholds.*
—II CORINTHIANS 10:4 NIV

Influence. Like a warrior princess who knows that one day she'll be needed for battle, this is what God's been grooming you for since the day you were born. Purpose is about influence or nothing at all. Influence isn't about reach or notoriety; it's about impact. And it's your impact that most frightens the enemy. Your gifts and your voice are what activate your superpowers. The more you step into your calling and embrace your anointing, the more it may feel as if you're under attack. You're a target of the enemy because you're a threat to the enemy. But take heart, for God has already overcome the enemy and you are fully protected by God's covering. Your beauty and influence are amplified by the wealth of wisdom, imagination, and potential inside you. The battle, then, is believing that you are indeed capable, worthy, and victorious. When we believe with authority, we become a miracle waiting to happen— and a supernatural weapon able to take out the darkness, doubt, disease, and despair. You are a daughter of the Most High…a natural-born warrior princess being recruited at this very moment for kingdom service. You are a weapon, beautiful but deadly.

What impact do you feel you're here to have, and what strongholds do you believe God has designed you to tear down?

_____

_____

_____

_____

_____

_____

_____

_____

_____

_____

_____

_____

_____

_____

_____

_____

PRAY

Lord, You've made me in Your image—a supernatural weapon fully equipped to defeat the enemy by being an extension of Your love, grace, forgiveness, anointing, and creativity. Continue to cover me as I go where You guide.

AMEN.

You Are Multifaceted

For the one whom God has sent
speaks the words of God,
for God gives the Spirit without limit.
—JOHN 3:34 NIV

It is not God's intent that we simply read about miraculous encounters in a Book that is thousands of years old. He intends that we be the Book, the living Word, a living manifestation of God's unlimited abilities and promises. In Romans 9:17 NIV, God says, "I raised you up for this very purpose, that I might display My power in you and that My name might be proclaimed in all the earth." At times you may feel too flawed for the big vision God has given you—or even overwhelmed by the various paths and possibilities. You're a masterpiece...and an essential component in God's master plan. Your magnificence isn't meant to be one-dimensional. No, you have multiple gifts, talents, and abilities, complete with endless opportunities. You're created in the image of our unlimited God. It's time to unapologetically step into your gifts, unleash your superpowers, and give credence to your dreams and desires. After all, God gave them to you. You'll never know or even be able to comprehend all that God has in store for you. Walking with God is a never-ending adventure—one where we never stop discovering how He's handcrafted us in His unlimited image and purpose.

Take a moment to do a "blessing dump." List the gifts, talents, unique insights, personality traits, and abilities God's given you to bless others.

Lord, help me to embrace the limitlessness of who I am
in You and how You've designed me for destiny.
Give me focus, discipline, curiosity, and mastery.
AMEN.

Prevailing Purpose

Many are the plans in a person's heart,
but it is the LORD's purpose that prevails.
—PROVERBS 19:21 NIV

In life, the only constant is change. And as confident as some may seem, none of us really know what God has in store. No matter how successful or spiritual we are, and no matter how accustomed we've grown to living for God, we'll never fully know every aspect of our purpose. Not while we're in this container called the human body. Walking with God is a never-ending adventure—one where we never stop discovering how He's handcrafted us in His unlimited image. Purpose can't be contained. Plus, God isn't seeking to give us certainty and results alone. He is first seeking to give us connection and relationship. In order to get us into alignment with our divine assignment, God will allow disruption into our lives. To be clear, disruption is an unexpected, inconvenient moment—an interruption necessary for course correction. These are life-altering and defining events. While disruption may seem like punishment, it's really an invitation for realignment. Disruption is designed to reposition us, elevate us, and propel us into stronger, wiser, and more anointed versions of ourselves.

How might God be using disruption to realign your plans for His greater purpose?

Lord, give me enough courage to embrace the changes
I do not desire or understand. I want what You want.
May Your purpose prevail over my preferences.

AMEN.

Desert Seasons

They did not thirst when he led them through the deserts;
he made water flow for them from the rock;
he split the rock and water gushed out.
—ISAIAH 48:21 NIV

Disruption is indeed an equal-opportunity employer. Being a follower of Christ does not somehow exempt us from hardship or seasons where it seems as if we're wandering alone in a desert wasteland. To the contrary, the pathway to higher purpose and promise almost always travels through a valley of pain...the desert. Perhaps it seems like others have abandoned you or severely disappointed you. What happened may have been unfair or downright evil, but God uses everything as a necessary part of your faith journey. There are some dimensions of inner destiny that can only be developed via difficulty. It's not punishment; it's preparation and realignment. When we shift our perspective, hardship is like weight that builds muscle, endurance, and strength. The good news is that you're never alone. You're never deserted. You're being developed for a greater deployment.

How has a recent disappointment chipped away at your faith? How is God inviting you to shift your perspective and see a bigger message and mission at work?

_____

_____

_____

_____

_____

_____

_____

_____

_____

_____

_____

_____

_____

_____

_____

_____

PRAY

Lord, help me to wear situations loosely. I'm not entitled to have things go my way. Build in me the type of spiritual insight that sees Your hand in the middle of every hardship.

AMEN.

Continuous Covering

Have I not commanded you?
Be strong and courageous.
Do not be afraid; do not be discouraged,
for the Lord your God will be with you
wherever you go.
—JOSHUA 1:9 NIV

When disruption bulldozes our doorstep and flips our lives upside down, it seems impossible to be strong and courageous. And this verse can feel like a lot of pressure to be perfect in the midst of difficulty, but it's really a promise. Nothing catches God by surprise...nothing is too difficult for God to navigate...and nothing is bigger than God. When people betray, disappoint, and abandon us—or when circumstances cut to the very core of our faith and hope—it's in this place that God promises an increased endowment of His presence. It is in God's presence that we find everything. The Spirit of God contains an endless supply of provision, possibility, pathways, purpose, and power. For this reason, we need not be afraid. It's okay to be shaken. It's okay to grieve and even be shell-shocked. That doesn't make you flawed; that makes you someone ready for supernatural revelation, support, healing, and focus. God doesn't abandon us the way imperfect people and unpredictable circumstances do. He's longing to elevate you into a new dimension of assurance that comes from going deeper in His Word and presence. You are covered. God is with you now and wherever you go.

Day 33

What disappointment do you need to give to God in exchange for more of His presence and peace?

_____

PRAY

*Lord, You are perfect in every way.
You are with me in this moment and guiding me deeper
into Your peace and power-filled presence.*

AMEN.

Identity Shifts

Do not be afraid, for I have ransomed you.
I have called you by name; you are Mine.
—ISAIAH 43:1 NLT

We can miss who we're called to be because we're addicted to or attached to who we've decided to be. Most of us women tend to define ourselves in one of five areas I call *The Five Success Mountains*. Each "mountain" simply represents a lane that we choose to live in and gives us a sense of identity. Number 1 is the *Marriage Mountain*. This is where we find our identity and sufficiency in being a wife and having a successful marriage that others admire. Number 2 is the *Motherhood Mountain*. This is where our identity is attached to our children. Number 3 is the *Money Mountain*. Here we find our worth in our work, the titles we earn, the check we make, the suits we wear, the offices we hold, the awards we win, the perceived impact we have, and how impressive we look. Number 4 is the *Mending Mountain*. Here we find validation in being able to help others solve their problems, being dependable, and sacrificing ourselves for the sake of saving others. And number 5 is the *Making a Difference Mountain*. This is where our core identity gets defined by the act of serving. Though our efforts seem noble, truly we want something in exchange—validation. You may identify with one or more of the mountains. None are bad. In fact, all are blessed. However, fixed beliefs about ourselves block us from God's master purpose. And for this reason, when God gets ready to shift you, you can guarantee He'll disrupt you.

To which mountain do you gravitate to most? How has it defined you or even confined you?

_____

_____

_____

_____

_____

_____

_____

_____

_____

_____

_____

_____

_____

_____

_____

_____

_____

_____

PRAY

Lord, I welcome disruption because it positions me for greater destiny and capacity. Show me where You're taking me. I know it is great and mighty.

AMEN.

Elevated Destiny

From the ends of the earth I call to you,
I call as my heart grows faint;
lead me to the rock that is higher than I.
—PSALM 61:2 NIV

Change is God's specialty, and interruption is God's area of mastery. We must always remember that God is more concerned with our character and capacity than He is our calling. We can become so obsessed with doing a work *for* God that we forget to become *who* God needs first. The Lord is always seeking to take us higher, but that will always require that we dig deeper. Our capacity to handle the calling upon our lives is too great and important for us to arrive at our destination underdeveloped. If you've been feeling like there is more, and if you're looking for God to show you more so that He can use you more, know that He will answer that prayer and longing with a master class in becoming more. That will require us to leave the familiar places and sometimes the people we cling to. And it means that disruption will be inconvenient and not always pleasant. Instead of fighting it, we should flow with it. There is wisdom waiting for you in the shift—and a depth of character and anointing ready to be deposited. The "rock that is higher than I" refers to a place of maturity and supernatural establishment. It is a firm yet elevated foundation upon which we can build God's higher purpose. Let this be a time that you ask God to lead you to a new place—to a rock that is much higher than your comfort, your current identity, and your comprehension.

When you think of God leading you to a rock that is higher than you, what comes to mind?

_____

_____

_____

_____

_____

_____

_____

_____

_____

_____

_____

_____

_____

_____

_____

_____

PRAY

*Lord, I refuse to be afraid of heights when I know
that You are holding my hand. Take me deeper and
develop my capacity for glorifying You at a higher level.*
AMEN.

Navigating Transition

*I will teach you and tell you the way to go
and how to get there; I will give you good counsel,
and I will watch over you.*
—PSALM 32:8 THE VOICE

Before a major life shake-up happens, usually God has been trying to get our attention for quite some time. Most of us don't like change. We love predictability and a good plan and a checklist and strategy to follow. We wrestle with God for the steering wheel. On one hand we want God to drive, but at the same time we secretly want to know what He's doing, where He's going, and how He plans on getting us there. But then disruption comes in and changes everything. It disturbs our attachment to predictability and anything that has too much of our heart and attention. Disruption is God's greatest classroom. This is one of the ways that He teaches us who we really are, what we're really made of, and how He intends for us to impact others in a greater way. To that end, disruption is both a teacher and a navigation system guiding us from our comfort zone to our glory zone—by taking us through what feels like a war zone. It's really a growth zone. When disruption hits, this is a time to lean in and seek God's heart; to ask for patience, perspective, and endurance; and to believe bigger than the obstacle in front of you. Take refuge in the irrevocable promise God has made to watch over and lead you.

What lessons might God be using disruption to teach you right now?

Lord, Your ways are better than mine.
Instead of fear and frustration, give me the mindset and heart
I need to navigate transition with forward-focused faith.

AMEN.

Birthing Bigger

"For I know the plans I have for you," declares the LORD,
"plans to prosper you and not to harm you,
plans to give you hope and a future."
—JEREMIAH 29:11 NIV

Babies come out crying because they're mad! They've not known anything other than the comfortable warmth of the womb. The unfamiliar is almost always unwanted…at least initially. And there is nothing pretty about birthing. Even deliveries without the intense pain aren't pretty—beautiful but not pretty. It's messy. Most things that matter are. But this is how the shift into higher purpose works. We get evicted from *here* and relocated *there*. God won't bless you *here* with what He has for you *there*. If He gave you your *there* blessing, you'd never move from *here*. You'd stay. So sometimes the reason God seems like He isn't answering your prayers is that the provision doesn't fit with where you are. God isn't being mean; He is being a parent. You never learn how to walk unless you take forward steps. If you're always carried, or if everything comes to you, then you never find your legs. You never learn what it takes to get up from where you are to get to where you could and should be. God isn't holding your blessing hostage; He has just put it *there*—smack in the center of the place He wants to get you to. However, the place in between your *here* and *there* is an obscure place of transition. God is intentionally moving you from the womb to the birth canal. It may be tight, dark, and uncomfortable, but you can't stay in the incubator forever. Embrace the shift. The best is on the other side of birth.

If you were to push through the discomfort of your current season, what do you imagine God might have for you on the other side?

Lord, help me to believe beyond where I've been and what I've done. Move me from here to there. I'm built for this journey.

AMEN.

Embracing Process

These trials will show that your faith is genuine.
It is being tested as fire tests and purifies gold—
though your faith is far more precious than mere gold.
So when your faith remains strong through many trials,
it will bring you much praise and glory and honor on the day when
Jesus Christ is revealed to the whole world.
—I PETER 1:7 NLT

Alignment with God's will is necessary for our divine assignment. Disruption gives us a chance to get an overdue adjustment while God brings all the skewed parts of our life into proper, powerful, and purpose-ready order. Think of it like going to the chiropractor—it's about getting aligned the way it's supposed to be. In the middle of the discomfort, it's important to remember that higher purpose is always on the other side of process. God sends His promise by way of a process, which is why we miss it! We think it is going to fall out of the sky like manna from heaven, but navigating *the Gap*—the zone of growth, transition, and divine reinvention—is where we must go to enter our promised land. Our purpose, more provision, more healing, and even more miracles are all on the other side of this process. *The Gap* is your wilderness between Egypt (what you've known) and the Promised Land (what you've been praying for and are destined for). What we're moving toward is not necessarily a bigger house, more money, less stress, or better relationships…although I have no doubt that everything is better on the other side of surrender. God doesn't leave our heart's desires behind as He ushers us into our destiny. But this isn't about stuff. It's about exchanging your current plans for the life God is calling you toward. And it's about getting where God needs you to accomplish something new that heaven is seeking to do.

What are some of the things God is asking you to release, unlearn, and do so that you're ready for your promised land?

Lord, help me to see the bigger picture
when the present moment is challenging my faith.
I lay down my plans for Your process and purpose.

AMEN.

False Goliaths

Stop judging by mere appearances,
but instead judge correctly.
—JOHN 7:24 NIV

Remember the story of David and Goliath? That was a personal battle—not because the two knew each other or were close friends (they weren't), but because they were in close proximity to each other. The battle was about something larger than both of them. However, the unique thing God showed us is how close the two were in terms of space and physical proximity. Sometimes it is those closest to us that can seem to hurt us the most. Betrayal…rejection…disappointment…it all stings. Know that God doesn't bless a mess. He doesn't bless messy objectives. And He doesn't bless your need, nor someone else's need, to be right and prove someone wrong. The battle isn't about the battle; it's about something bigger. Goliath was called a giant because of his size, but he was easily taken out because he lacked substance. Don't let something that seems big cause you to forget who you are, *whose* you are, and the spiritual DNA you possess. To be a physical giant is far less important than being a spiritual giant. A spiritual giant is someone in whom God's might and power lives. Spiritual giants are extensions of God's hands and heart. No one is immune from trouble. In fact, we are guaranteed to have it. But we must also remember that God has already overcome every obstacle we could face. Don't let a visible giant stop you from seeing the unseen hand of God at work in your life. Things aren't always as they seem.

Day 39

What fake giants are you facing right now? How have you let their presence fool you?

PRAY

Lord, may Your spirit guide me, guard me,
and grow the real spiritual giant within me.
AMEN.

Beyond Betrayal

...and they plotted to arrest Jesus
in some sly way and kill Him..
—MATTHEW 26:4

Betrayal is one of the best teachers in God's syllabus. No one knew this better than Jesus. He loved. He served. He even allowed people close to Him to betray Him. One reason He did was so that Scripture would be fulfilled and confirm God's master will and plan for mankind. Another reason was to show that betrayal happens to all of us. No matter who you are, people will disappoint you, let you down, and violate your trust. That doesn't make it okay, but it also doesn't mean that you're hopelessly flawed either. On the contrary, betrayal is often a form of disruption that God may not send but one He will use to reveal and develop our heart condition. Do we have the capacity to pray for someone who hurt us? Will we hold a grudge? Will we forgive? And will we let bitterness and regret take root in our lives and grow into distrust, isolation, and low esteem? God has a plan for you bigger than betrayal. Do not forget that nothing catches Him by surprise. Hold fast to a higher vision and belief in the greater mission that God is preparing you for right now. Have more faith in your future than what feels like a failure. And, remember, sometimes we have to see a snake to know what one looks like.

What are some of the blessings you can find in the midst of betrayal?

Lord, give me a healed heart that lets go
of what no longer belongs in my life. Make me a graceful
and courageous navigator of change,
such that my blessings and burdens all bring You glory.
AMEN.

The Faith Formula

And all things, whatsoever ye shall ask in prayer,
believing, ye shall receive.
—MATTHEW 21:22 KJV

I read twenty versions of this particular Scripture one day. Initially, it's easy to make "Ask. Believe. Receive" as the faith formula we take away. That's not exactly what this verse teaches. It's really "Believe. Ask. Receive." Indeed, prayer is the pathway to the heart of God. When there's a lot to hope for or when things are not going the way we'd like, we become skilled at asking. But the real test is in the believing. If prayer is the pathway, *BELIEF* is what enables our petition to pass through. Let that soak in for a moment. We've been taught to "ask and then it shall be given." We've been told to "name it and claim it." And we've been taught that "you have not because you ask not." But this passage makes clear that our prayers must be bathed in belief first. Belief is an activator. Know that God hears the prayers of those who believe what they are praying for.

Are there areas where you've been praying from a place of disbelief? How do you fear that God won't come through for you?

_____

_____

_____

_____

_____

_____

_____

_____

_____

_____

_____

_____

_____

_____

_____

_____

_____

_____

PRAY

Dear Lord, remove from me the spirits of fear, disbelief, hesitation, worry, and doubt. These voices don't come from You and therefore don't belong to me. Give me a spirit of crazy faith and the ability to trust in You no matter what I see.

AMEN.

Power over Potential

Are you so foolish?
After beginning with the Spirit,
are you now trying to attain your goal
by human effort?
—GALATIANS 3:3

Walking with God is a spiritual journey that unfolds in the realm of earth. Every day we have decisions to make and responsibilities to attend to. It's easy for the lines of faith and flesh to subtly blur. When we believe God for something, we're asking Him to show up in our lives in very practical ways. We're asking Him to bless the works of our hands, to order our steps, and to give us the ability to steward, perform, and live well. So when God equips us and we become proficient, we can begin to feel like it is us doing the doing. When we fall into the deception of self-reliance, however, we can become addicted to our own abilities. Eventually that breeds stress and pride. The passage above reminds us that it is foolish to try to thrive by human effort alone. Foolish doesn't mean evil—it just means unwise. But wisdom comes from having experience and understanding. God is inviting you to have a radical faith adventure with Him...to experience supernatural trust that only comes when we stretch our belief and enter into new territories. He wants us to learn what it feels like to lean on Him as opposed to ourselves. It is by His Spirit that your dreams and desires will come to fruition.

In what areas are you relying upon human effort because you're struggling to believe that God will come through for you?

Lord, thank You for equipping me with Your DNA
and limitless abilities. Help me to never trust my potential
more than I do Your power.

AMEN.

Security in God's Promise

I declare from the beginning how it will end and foretell
from the start what has not yet happened. I decree that
my purpose will stand, and I will fulfill my every plan.
—ISAIAH 46:10

We change our minds every single day—sometimes multiple times throughout the day. As human beings, God has made us wonderfully complex, for sure. And that complexity often makes us indecisive. We think about everything, weighing the pros and cons, and we evaluate the likelihood of outcomes and possibilities. But God doesn't think or operate the way we do! To the contrary, God says, "For My thoughts are not your thoughts, neither are your ways My ways....As the heavens are higher than the earth, so are My ways higher than your ways and My thoughts than your thoughts" (Isaiah 55:8–9 NIV). In order for us to believe the promises of God, we have to first trust the character, nature, and unchanging essence of God. When God promises, He proves. He provides. And He follows through. Every purpose He has for you will stand. It cannot be thwarted. And every element of His plan will be fulfilled. How? That part is none of our business. Our job is to believe, to be obedient, and to step when and wherever He steers. This is a season that is going to require you to believe the promises of God like never before. You believe the blessing into being.

What promise or whisper from God have you struggled to believe will actually come to fruition?

_____
_____
_____
_____
_____
_____
_____
_____
_____
_____
_____
_____
_____
_____
_____
_____
_____
_____
_____

PRAY

Lord, I thank You for being a secure place for me
to invest my trust and my heart's desires. You are unchanging.
You mean what You say. Align my thoughts, my will,
my purpose, and my plans with Yours.

AMEN.

Focusing Forward

I press toward the mark for the prize
of the high calling of God in Christ Jesus.
—PHILIPPIANS 3:14 KJV

Everything fresh that God has for you is ahead. We are to learn from the past, but we cannot live there. God's mercies, gifts, and blessings are new each and every day. It's wonderful to celebrate the good and give God praise, but we also must be careful not to romanticize the past. Otherwise we'll neglect the gifts of the present and miss the pathway into the future. Pressing on toward the mark of the prize of the *high* calling means that we focus forward. Release what and who didn't work out. It's time to operate in your expectation, not your experience. There is something sweeter on the horizon, but we must believe it to seize it. It's time to shed the wounds and worries and raise your faith and expectancy. That's the only way to enter the new dimension and promised land God has specifically for you.

How have you been putting your faith in or living in your past experiences versus in faith-stretching expectations?

Lord, thank You for what You've brought me through. Prepare my heart, mind, and spirit for the future You're taking me to.

AMEN.

Entering the Spectacular

Let us seize and hold tightly the confession
of our hope without wavering, for He who promised
is reliable and trustworthy and faithful [to His word].
—HEBREWS 10:23 AMP

Too often we hold onto what was. Other times we cling relentlessly unto what is. But next-level faith means that we hold onto what we believe, not what we've seen or where we've been. The past can be a pit that pulls us backward—longing for the good ol' days or a chance to do things over. The present is indeed a gift, but it also doesn't contain the fullness of what is ahead. For this reason, we are to anchor our belief in a never-ending hope. God desires that we appreciate our journey, grow from our experiences, and live fully in the gift of the present moment. But He also desires that we live expectantly...eagerly anticipating heaven's next move, your next invitation, and goodness that is always on its way to you. If we cling too tightly to the familiar, we block ourselves from perceiving and entering the spectacular. God is faithful; that is not up for debate. But the question is, do we believe that supernatural goodness is indeed on the way? Know that God has an infinite number of ways—far beyond your comprehension—to bless you, guide you, heal you, and fulfill His every promise and plan for you too.

How does holding onto what was (or how you think things should be) prevent you from fully believing in something bigger?

PRAY

Lord, there is no limit to what You can and will do.
Give me spiritual eyes that see beyond what is and a heart
that eagerly anticipates Your guidance, goodness, and grace.
AMEN.

Magnificent Thinking

Finally, believers, whatever is true, whatever is honorable
and worthy of respect, whatever is right and confirmed by
God's Word, whatever is pure and wholesome, whatever is lovely
and brings peace, whatever is admirable and of good repute;
if there is any excellence, if there is anything
worthy of praise, think continually on these things
[center your mind on them, and implant them in your heart].
—PHILIPPIANS 4:8 AMP

So often our thoughts can become hijacked by the warnings and lazy words of other people. It may seem like wisdom, but it's really just limiting beliefs filled with fear, regret, and passed-down sayings that are not anchored in God's truth or intention. The Bible tells us to think of very specific things from above, not obsess over the advice or opinions of others. And it does not say that we should accept circumstances as they are to guide our thoughts of what's possible in the future. Instead, the Word tells exactly what to think about. Think about things that are pure, true, worthy of respect, and what is confirmed by God's Word. Our thoughts make way for our feelings, and our feelings influence our choices, perceptions, and, ultimately, our beliefs. We are what we believe. So let us not be lazy or casual with our thoughts. And let us not come into agreement with messages of doom and gloom, sickness, or difficulty. Center your mind on the magnificent.

What old sayings and passed-down opinions have lured you into believing that life is hard as opposed to magnificent?

_____

_____

_____

_____

_____

_____

_____

_____

_____

_____

_____

_____

_____

_____

_____

_____

PRAY

Lord, I come out of agreement with any thought
that doesn't line up with Your Word. Thank You
for equipping me to experience the impossible.

AMEN.

Power of Words

*Your words are so powerful
that they will kill or give life,
and the talkative person will reap
the consequences.*
—PROVERBS 18:21 TPT

One of the most powerful tools God has given us to co-architect an abundant life is found in our words. Our words are more powerful than we realize. When we speak, it's like a signal that goes out and invites back what we've asked for into our lives, almost like a boomerang. Our words are also like soldiers who accomplish their mission. We see in Scripture that Jesus spoke to a fig tree, and with His words, the fig tree withered. Jesus spoke to the storm and commanded the wind and seas to settle. And God spoke the world into being when He said, "Let there be light" (Genesis 1:3 NIV). Words can create something out of nothing. Your words, therefore, must be treated like strategic assets. You have the God-given authority (in Jesus's name) to declare healing, peace, and strength. But you can't allow your feelings, fears, or sight to shape what you say. Your words have *resurrection* power. Remember, Jesus spoke to Lazarus and brought him back to life. You, too, have been gifted with the power of the tongue. Use it wisely. Think about what you desire and then declare it so. Speak what you seek until you see what you've said.

How have you been inviting difficulty into your life because of speaking negatively or from a place of fear?

_____

_____

_____

_____

_____

_____

_____

_____

_____

_____

_____

_____

_____

_____

_____

_____

PRAY

God, I believe that You are doing a great work in me, around me, and for me. I declare that excellence, abundance, and wellness are my portion now and forever. In Jesus's name,

AMEN.

Impossibly Possible

I am the LORD, the God of all mankind.
Is anything too hard for Me?
—JEREMIAH 32:27 NIV

The Bible tells us in Proverbs 23:7 NKJV, "For as he thinks in his heart, so is he." That means that our thoughts reflect who we are. For that reason, miracles are a mindset. So often in Scripture we see Jesus telling those in need of healing that they need only believe. The life of Jesus is designed to show us how to live life in a realm where miracles freely flow. When we spend significant time in the presence of God, we can better experience His thoughts, peace, and leading. God is always leading you to a blessing or a breakthrough. Miracles are all around…but we cannot access what we don't believe. And the great news is that you need not be perfect. God looks for surrendered trust, not perfection. He does not need ideal circumstances or anyone's permission to bless you. Nothing is stronger than the mighty hand of God. God alone is writing your story, not you. Not your haters either. God can use anything and anyone to bless you at any given moment. In fact, it's what He loves to do.

What area of your life seems impossible? How is God using this to invite a new level of belief and trust?

_____
_____
_____
_____
_____
_____
_____
_____
_____
_____
_____
_____
_____
_____
_____
_____
_____
_____
_____

PRAY

Lord, I know that You can do all things.
Nothing is too hard for you. I am a magnet for miracles
and a vessel for Your glory.

AMEN.

On the Other Side

But as for you, be strong and do not give up,
for your work will be rewarded.
—II CHRONICLES 15:7 NIV

Obstacles can seem like a sign that we're on the wrong path, or they can make us feel as if something is inherently wrong with us. But the truth is, God uses obstacles to strengthen us the way weights build muscle. He is less concerned with what's happening in your life and more concerned with how you're approaching life. What if the obstacle you're facing right now was an invitation to believe bigger? Every chance to believe bigger and live bolder will be faced with resistance, doubt, and difficulty. It's not a reflection of your brokenness; it's actually a clue as to the greater resilience, brilliance, and dominance that God is seeking to build within you. We can't always dictate our circumstances, but we *can* control how we face them. So if you've hit a wall, don't give up. Your breakthrough is on the other side, and the process is building something powerful and necessary within. God requires progress, not perfection. He longs to travel this road intimately with you. This is a chance for you to hear His voice like never before—and a chance to discover a higher version of you that will never emerge if you allow the obstacle to trick you into stopping, second-guessing, or retreating. Get up. Keep pressing. Try again. God is just getting started.

Where is God telling you not to give up and to try again?

God, You have placed victory in my DNA.
Order my footsteps. Guide me through the difficulty and
into a majestic destiny that I know is waiting for me.

AMEN.

Inner Faith, Outer Flow

Whoever believes in Me, as Scripture has said,
rivers of living water will flow from within them.
—JOHN 7:38 NIV

When you think about a river, you may think of a stream that leads into a larger body of water like a pond, lake, or ocean. All water is not created equal. In fact, stagnant water is toxic. Water needs to flow. Jesus uses a river to explain one of the greatest gifts of being a believer in and a carrier of the Spirit of Jesus Christ. He didn't just say we'd be full of water, no. He specifically decreed that multiple streams of living water will flow from within us when we believe. The distinction is important. So often we misconstrue faith to be about believing God for something to come *to* us, but Jesus promised something greater. We have the endowment of supernatural anointing already *within* us for the purpose of giving life. Faith is about trusting that the Holy Spirit will move from the inside out—that God would equip you with the mind you need to solve a problem; that *He* would replenish your cells for healing to happen internally; and that you would be a source of life-giving and -refreshing to others, not just a receiver or reservoir. Oh, how wonderful it would be for us to shift our perspective to embrace the abundant life that Jesus says lives within as opposed to looking outside ourselves for what He has already given us. When we believe that we matter and unapologetically own that God has given us a special endowment for His higher purpose, we understand that the larger body of water we're feeding into is the ocean of God's love, master plan, and glory.

How does the notion of being a carrier of living water flowing from you help you to understand your identity and purpose?

_____
_____
_____
_____
_____
_____
_____
_____
_____
_____
_____
_____
_____
_____
_____
_____
_____
_____

PRAY

*Lord, I believe in You, and I believe in what You've prebuilt me
to do. I am a vessel and a carrier of supernatural goodness.
Let it flow from within me in exponential ways.*

AMEN.

Self-Doubt

The wise woman builds her house,
but with her own hands the foolish one tears hers down.
—PROVERBS 14:1 NIV

Eventually, limiting beliefs, fears, insecurities, and behaviors become *blessing blockers*—self-sabotaging habits that get ingrained into our personality, attitudes, outlook, and choices. We end up blocking our own blessings and self-dismantle our dreams and desires. There are a ton of 'em, but we'll talk about the most common blockers that keep us stuck and also how God wants us to believe bigger than what we've been through and what we're used to.

Let's tackle self-doubt first. Doubt and destiny are like two sides of a coin. Most of our self-doubt comes from the opinions, expectations, and wounds of others passed down as wisdom. We've been taught to believe in God but never taught how to believe in ourselves in a healthy and hearty way. When lingering inner thoughts whisper that we're not good enough, loved enough, worthy enough...or just *enough*, we shrink. We settle. And we self-sabotage. The Scripture above depicts how self-sabotage unfolds. On one hand, a woman builds what she believes she can attain or even deserves. But on the other hand, the same woman tears down the house that she just built. Who would consciously do such a thing? Proverbs is letting us know that both wisdom and folly are in our DNA. We will never fully pursue what we don't believe we're worthy to receive. And so with our own hands, we tear down blessings, relationships, and opportunities. Doubting yourself is really doubting God. To believe bigger means to believe that you're worthy, wonderful, and ready.

In what areas do you doubt God will use you, bless you, heal you, restore you, shift you, or come through for you?

Lord, remove double-mindedness from me.
Take my negative thoughts captive and
replace them with fearless focus and faith.
AMEN.

Isolation

As iron sharpens iron,
so one person sharpens another.
—PROVERBS 27:17 NIV

Isolation is really a fear of trusting others. Prolonged solitude is the soil of self-doubt. It can be a threat to your faith and life's mission—and become a breeding ground where fear is able to run wild with whispers of lack and insecurity, as well. As intimate as a walk with God is, it's not meant to be done alone. We most often distance ourselves from others when trust is broken. However, when people let us down, we can also make unhealthy vows to never let that kind of disappointment enter our lives again. We can allow a spirit of distrust to enter our hearts. In doing so, we bring the past into the present, and that pollutes our future. Skepticism and mistrust aren't the same as discernment, though we often try to dress them up as such. They're just another excuse to stay to ourselves as opposed to risk the vulnerability found in trusting others. Isolation is a trap. God wants us to be in community with others, especially other women who can support our growth. Look at Mary and Elizabeth: they both needed each other during a precious time of pregnancy that required a circle of faith. Plus, our lives are intentionally interconnected. The very wisdom you need to make your shift will likely come from a messenger you're least likely to expect or appreciate.

How has betrayal or disappointment created distrust or caused you to pull away from others? What will you do to course-correct?

Lord, You've not designed me to operate with fear in any area of my life. Surround me with a sound circle of love, wisdom, and boldness.

AMEN.

Comparison

Let's just go ahead and be what we were made to be,
without enviously or pridefully comparing ourselves
with each other, or trying to be something we aren't.
—ROMANS 12:6 THE MESSAGE

As hard as it may be to believe, what God is doing in the lives of others has absolutely nothing to do with what He is seeking to do in you! Comparison cripples our confidence and compromises our calling. When we obsess about what others are doing, more limiting beliefs enter our mind and the spirit of fear gets to whispering: "You're not doing enough. You're behind. It's too late. You're not as talented. Your life isn't as pretty. You don't have enough. You just aren't enough." Media images stir up the spirit of comparison every day. We see airbrushed images of children who don't cry and women who wake up with perfect lashes, flawless skin, and lots of vacations. While you're working, trying to pay the bills, keep the kids from tearing each other apart, and somehow squeeze in a bath, it seems as if everyone else is living a perfect life. Remember, the enemy will indeed use anything to exploit an insecurity that already exists. The other danger of comparison is ego. It can lead to competition and arrogance. We can start to feel like we're better than others because our life seems to be better. Or, in an attempt to keep up, we start striving, proving, and showing off. No matter how you slice it or dice it, there is nothing good that comes from comparison. God wants us to look up, not around.

How has comparison crippled your courage, clarity, or confidence?

Lord, keep my eyes focused on You
and on the plans you have for me.
I will embrace my lane, my gifts, and my assignment.
AMEN.

Indecision

If you wait for perfect conditions,
you will never get anything done.
—ECCLESIASTES 11:4 TLB

Prayer is essential, but it can become another hideout—an excuse not to make a bigger, bolder decision. If you find yourself afraid to move until you hear God speak, that is still fear. And God has not given us a spirit of fear (II Timothy 1:7 NKJV). But what if good is good enough for God's grace to make up the distance? What if God speaks most powerfully by saying nothing at all? The belief that we have to get it right or we'll somehow step out of grace stems from the fear that if we're not careful, we're going to mess up our lives. Or mess up someone else's life. Or severely disappoint God to the point that we'll have to face His wrath. That's our real guiding belief. It's a subtle but toxic form of perfectionism that pollutes our ability to use the mind that God gave us.

We overthink, over-pray, and over-research our way out of blessed opportunities. And we over-question, trying to discern whether something is God's will. God desires that we become leapers instead of watchers. Also, God never said we should wait for the perfect time. He wants us to trust *His* timing, which is almost always inconvenient and intimidating. Perhaps it's time to do what God has already said, to do what's already written in His Word, to meet a need we can already see! We don't need to hyper-spiritualize the obvious. We won't know 100 percent of the time exactly what God's will is. And we don't have to look for confirmation in every possible avenue. That's fear, not faith.

How does fear tend to show up as indecision in your life?

Lord, give me an undivided heart.
Guide me in the way that I should go
with boldness, decisiveness, and surrender.

AMEN.

Facts

Here is a boy
with five small barley loaves and two small fish,
but how far will they go among so many?
—JOHN 6:9 NIV

Facts may be true, but they aren't necessarily the whole truth. God operates in the unseen. That is the very nature of God—to create something out of nothing. God is not limited by anything; miracles are His domain. And God loves to surprise us. Believing only in what we can see, quantify, and prove is often just a way that the spirit of fear gets us to embrace a rational lie. The enemy loves to rationalize—to twist facts and tell half truths—or, as I say, to spew rational-lies. Because God operates in the unseen realm and because His provision is limitless, facts don't tell the full picture—especially when God is writing the story. Remember the little boy with two fish and five loaves of bread and thousands of hungry people? Facts said there was no way that food was enough for thousands of people...but it was. God creates things out of nothing. Facts have little to do with how real faith and supernatural manifestation work. A key secret to a major life shift is speaking faith and not facts. When we trust in the unseen and expect what we haven't experienced, that's the very invitation God responds to—and this is the type of next-level, bigger belief needed to enter and experience the incredible.

Day 55

What facts have been blocking you from seeing what God is actually saying, revealing, and doing?

Hoarding

He sets the time for finding and the time for losing,
the time for saving and the time for throwing away.
—ECCLESIASTES 3:6 GNT

So much of making a meaningful life shift is about emptying out. Our lives are full of clutter. Clutter can be physical stuff we're attached to that makes us feel or look important, or it can be achievements and accolades. It can be memories of the good ol' days. And it can be any place, prize, protocol, or people we cling to and find refuge or significance in. We can even hoard unforgiveness, regret, and cynicism. Hoarding is just another way we hold onto the old—the old ways of thinking, living, and finding significance. Whatever we hold onto the most has a hold on us. Our stubbornness most reflects our areas of distrust, and what we hoard ends up being what God asks us to surrender to Him. Clinging to what God needs you to release blocks the very space God needs to have available to bless you and build you in a bigger, better way. When we hold onto less than what God has for us, it lessens our lives and leaves us weighed down. Remember, God will not bless whatever He is trying to break.

Day 56

Can you think of something God is leading you to let go of?

_____

_____

_____

_____

_____

_____

_____

_____

_____

_____

_____

_____

_____

_____

_____

_____

_____

_____

_____

_____

PRAY

Lord, I give to you what no longer belongs
in my life, in head, heart, or hands.

AMEN.

Distraction

Look straight ahead,
and fix your eyes on what lies before you.
—PROVERBS 4:25 NLT

Focus is probably the most important skill you need to enter a bigger, (B)uilt (I)n (G)od future. Fear is a master of distraction. Distraction is the most effective weapon in fear's arsenal. Ever wonder why it's easy to finish the insignificant things but you procrastinate when it comes to your big dreams and desires? Distractions are a doozy. Dr. Fred Jones says, "Distractions are the death of your dreams happening in slow motion!" And distractions are intentional—a stealth form of resistance designed to block your bigger. The key to making a shift is to pay attention to the truly important things and to learn what (and who) to ignore. The greater the significance, the greater the resistance—and the more susceptible we are to self-sabotage, doubt, and succumbing to distractions. Even opportunity can be a distraction disguised as destiny. Not everything that looks good is necessary to God. When you're in a shift, it's especially key to be on the lookout for distractions, for they will be coming. When you get new opportunities, new ideas, and new invitations, ask whether these are in alignment with what you feel is God's new vision.

What distractions usually take you off course?

Lord, give me the discipline to discern and delete anything that takes me off the course of completion, calling, and character development.

AMEN.

People-Pleasing

Am I now trying to win the approval of human beings,
or of God? Or am I trying to please people? If I were
still trying to please people, I would not be a servant of Christ.
—GALATIANS 1:10 NIV

When a woman doesn't know her purpose, she settles. She settles for protocol, proving, perfectionism, appropriateness, and people-pleasing. There is nothing wrong with wanting people to be proud of you or to be celebrated and affirmed by others. But we enter into a dangerous realm when the desire for approval and validation becomes an addiction. Slowly but surely, we can begin to trade God's voice for the voices of others and their rules, ways, and affirmations. You may want someone else to see how hard you've worked or to merely accept you as you are. And you may be waiting for someone else to give you permission to want more, be more, and have more. But what if they don't? You can't expect anyone to honor your anointing if you don't, and it's unwise to give others power that doesn't belong in their hands. God already created you in His image. You don't need to chase after approval, nor do you need permission to do or be what God has already precommissioned. When you worry about what others will think, you move from faith into shadow-chasing. The fickle whims of others are always moving targets and never-ending pits. Jesus knew this full well. He let no one define Him. He left behind places where people lacked belief in who He was. He refused to conform to limiting beliefs, religiosity, and notions of appropriateness. That's why He spent so much time outside the four walls of the church and stayed in the trenches with everyday people. God wants you to ditch pleasing people for embracing your distinctiveness and unique calling too.

How have you been letting the need for approval and acceptance of your ideas, desires, or personality block you?

God, I live for an audience of One.
Detox me from the dirt of approval and people-pleasing.
Your validation is all I need.

AMEN.

Unforgiveness

Be kind to one another, tender-hearted, forgiving each other,
just as God in Christ also has forgiven you.
—EPHESIANS 4:32 NASB

Forgiveness is the only way forward. We might believe that, but it isn't always easy to do it, especially not right away after hurt visits. Don't let people or religiosity make you feel guilty because it doesn't happen in an instant. Deliverance isn't magic. And forgiveness can become a self-defeating obsession, especially when everyone is telling you over and over how you have to forgive, but no one tells you how to do it. Actually, forgiveness isn't about focusing on forgiveness. You'll feel like the right thing to do is pray about what happened to you. That's a trap. Here's the thing: *we have to shift from simply praying about the problem and instead start visualizing the solution.* The key to forgiveness is to shift from the pain to focusing on the future, promise, and possibility. Focusing on things above lifts us out of the ditch of despair and disappointment. Ask God to give you a new vision of yourself and make you a woman able to walk in forgiveness and trust, not bitterness. Pray for what you want to come to you. Don't keep rehearsing what's already been removed! We must keep committing to dumping out of our hearts the dirt left over by others. When we replay our worst memories, we re-wound our self-esteem and reanchor ourselves in the past. Replaying, masked as trying to forgive, is why it can be incredibly hard to get unstuck. Stop setting a time line. Be patient with yourself, yet still be intentional about how you approach each day. Stay focused daily on moving forward and onto a bigger vision and purpose. This is a better investment of your energy and puts you on the path of healing and elevation.

Instead of trying to forgive what happened to you, how can you focus forward on the bigger vision that God has for you?

*Lord, I accept what I can't explain
and ask for a vision bigger than blame.
I speak life into what I seek, not what I've seen.*

AMEN.

Shrinking

Do not think of yourself more highly than you ought,
but rather think of yourself with sober judgment,
in accordance with the faith God has distributed to each of you.
—ROMANS 12:3 NIV

Our trust in God is not somehow separate from our belief in ourselves. For far too long we've been taught that believing unapologetically in yourself is considered unladylike or unholy.

To the contrary, divine trust and self-belief are linked together by the umbilical cord of purpose. We cannot fulfill our destiny with just one or the other; we need both. The Bible says not to think *more* highly of yourself than you should, but it doesn't say *not* to think highly of yourself. The reason God wants you to have a strong, all-things-are-possible self-image is for the very purpose of you being able to fulfill your purpose. You need a healthy and hearty self-image to even have the audacity to pursue all God has in store for you. Notice that I didn't say you need a strong self-image to believe in God. It's not enough to be a woman who loves God but doesn't really like herself. That's not God's will. But truth be told, most of us as women spend an inordinate amount of our time trying to fix our faults or find a way to simply "live with" ourselves. If you don't learn to celebrate yourself, you'll settle for a life where you simply tolerate yourself. You'll shrink. You'll settle. You'll take the leftovers and never go after what God has for you. What if you really believed in your potential and power, not only your imperfections? There is nothing God-glorifying about you hiding your anointing, gifts, and voice. The very nature of your existence is a supernatural permission slip! When God said "Let there be light" (Genesis 1:3 NIV), He was giving you permission to shine.

Make a list of at least twenty-one things you love and appreciate about yourself.

PRAY

God, make me a woman who is unashamed of her magnificence.
Keep my heart pure, my gifts sharp, and my confidence
anchored unapologetically in you.

AMEN.

Intentional Incubation

Be still, and know that I am God;
I will be exalted among the nations,
I will be exalted in the earth.
—PSALM 46:10 NIV

Isn't it interesting that stillness was our first home but now it can seem oh so foreign and difficult to find? We start out in our mother's womb, a place of incubation and quiet perfection. But then something changed. We entered into a world full of noise, hustle, and bustle. When we're young, all we want is to be swaddled in sweet serenity. But now peace can be hard to harness. That's why God issues stillness as a command, not a request. He instructs us to *be still*—lovingly but firmly. Just as a mother speaks with both protection and passion to her offspring, seeking to keep him or her out of harm's way, God does the same thing to us. To be still requires us to be intentional. To enter into the womb of God's presence. To stop. To unplug. To connect to our Messiah through the umbilical cord of prayer and serene communion. Stillness is a success strategy—one that prepares us to receive the majestic and to be an usherer of miracles.

How has God been nudging you to slow down? How has this been a challenge for you?

_____

_____

_____

_____

_____

_____

_____

_____

_____

PRAY

Lord, the busyness of life always seems to squeeze its way into my head and heart. My mind tends to race and my hands feel idle if there is nothing to do. Help me to understand the "be" in Your command to "Be still." Help me to be an extension of Your Being as opposed to an unfocused doer. I long to be guided by Your goodness and grace. Teach me the power, purpose, and prosperousness found in entering divine stillness.
In Jesus's name, AMEN.

Inner Assurance

*Surrender your anxiety! Be silent and stop your striving
and you will see that I am God.
I am the God above all the nations,
and I will be exalted throughout the whole earth.*
—PSALM 46:10 TPT

Divine stillness is a byproduct of being anchored in God's presence. It's not about what you do; it's about how you do it. It's an inner essence. When we experience an inability to be still, there is something within us that's restless. It might seem minor, but it's actually major. Ultimately, it's a lack of trust. We feel that if we're not busy or in control, something is going to fall apart. You see, S.T.I.L.L. stands for (S)urrendered (T)rust (I)n the (L)ord's (L)eadership. We fight stillness because we're fighting for control. The second part in Psalm 46:10 that states *"and know"* is really critical. In life, we trust what and in whom we know. God is reminding us here that stillness is not only a command and a decision, but it's a place that we only enter into when we KNOW that God is God. Not intellectually but fully assured that God is faithful, infinitely wise, and well able. Stillness without belief and surrendered trust isn't possible.

What is it you're afraid will not work out in your favor? And what's the truth that fear doesn't want you to know?

PRAY

Father, give me a heart synced with where Your hands are leading. I thank You for the privilege of spending time with You. I trust You. I need You. You are my God.

AMEN.

Slow Miracles

For the LORD God is a sun and shield;
the Lord bestows favor and honor;
no good thing does He withhold from those
whose walk is blameless.
—PSALM 84:11 NIV

It's easy to celebrate the instant miracles—where healing comes quickly, answers flow like a river, or clarity comes within moments, not months. But what about when there is silence and slowness? What do you do when what you're praying for isn't producing any proof? We're *supposed* to keep the faith. In reality, we start thinking that something must be wrong with us or maybe even our prayers. And it can be difficult to see miracles happen *around* you while wondering if God is ever going to come through *for* you. I'm here to tell you today that heaven sees you. God hasn't forgotten about you. Our Savior isn't disappointed in you. In fact, God has something unique in store for you, but He won't rush it. The fast miracles may feel good, but the slow miracles will *feed* good. You are being equipped with manna that will feed others in limitless ways. You matter too much for God to give you an unfinished blessing. We must trust God with the slow miracles too.

How is God using what seems like a delay as a chance to develop something greater inside you? What might that something be and why?

_____

_____

_____

_____

_____

_____

_____

_____

_____

_____

_____

_____

_____

_____

_____

_____

_____

_____

PRAY

Lord, turn my impatience into endurance.
Give me the eyes to see and the faith to believe
that my miracle is already in progress.
I trust Your timing and master plan.

AMEN.

Hearing God's Voice

The one who sent Me is with Me;
He has not left Me alone,
for I always do what pleases Him.
—JOHN 8:29 NIV

Stillness is the most tried-and-true passageway into the supernatural sea of surrender. When we surrender, we're trading our will for God's way. It's an opportunity, not an obligation, to commit our plans to the Lord. Our yielding enables God's shielding. He *saves* us from ourselves and shields us from our blind spots. In the center of surrender is also a *showcase*. God shows us His proprietary plans and higher vision. In the stillness, He reveals what we cannot see when we're striving, busybody-proving and people-pleasing. And it is from a place of stillness and surrender that God most effectively *steers* us in the way we should go. God will not compete for your attention. Committing to moments of stillness is an act of worship and prioritization of God's agenda. We can't merely desire to please Him; we must also actively pursue Him. It's time to lose yourself in His presence so you can hear His voice and allow His heartbeat to direct the works of your hands.

How can you better incorporate stillness as a lifestyle?

Releasing Anxiousness

Be anxious for nothing, but in everything
by prayer and supplication, with thanksgiving,
let your requests be made known to God;
and the peace of God, which surpasses all understanding,
will guard your hearts and minds through Christ Jesus.
—PHILIPPIANS 4:6–7 NKJV

When God gives us a directive, He doesn't put an asterisk at the end. There is no fine print with exceptions and conditions where His Word and will don't apply. We are to be anxious for absolutely nothing. By anxious, God means that we are not to be worried, apprehensive, fearful, distressed, nervous, antsy, or on edge. God knows that we will have a tendency to default to our emotions, so He gives us a better way to handle them. We are to turn our angst into peace, prayer, and thanksgiving. But it takes *TRUST*—Total Reliance Upon Spiritual Timing—for that to happen. Really, the question is whether we believe that God hears us and is actively working on our behalf. When we doubt God's interest and commitment to our lives, we doubt God's timing. Doubt always opens the door to anxiety, restlessness, and misaligned decisions. However, when we believe that God is supreme and will perfect every single thing that concerns us, we gain the gift of peace that surpasses all understanding. And it is in this place that provision and pathways become uniquely clear.

What has made you anxious lately, and how does that shed light on how you doubt God?

_____

_____

_____

_____

_____

_____

_____

_____

_____

_____

_____

_____

_____

_____

_____

_____

_____

PRAY

Lord, give me a steadfast sense of trust in Your timing.
Remove all doubt and replace it with extreme reliance upon You.
AMEN.

Alone Time

My soul finds rest in God alone;
My salvation comes from Him.
—PSALM 62:1

Being in God's presence is such a gift—one available at all times. It's easy to go to others for answers to our problems or to unplug altogether to avoid difficulty. But there is nothing more enriching, healing, and replenishing than learning to rest in God alone. That means that God is the first place we should go to seek wisdom. It is wonderful to have the friendship and guidance of others, but we should never substitute a direct revelation from God with the secondhand advice of others. When we go to God first, we're aligning with the only One who knows our purpose, plans, and pathways. Sometimes the anxiousness we feel is because we've merely been nibbling on the crumbs left over by someone else's quiet time with God. Instead, God desires to impart something magnificent to us, directly and intimately with no filters, barriers, or interruptions. God is always after our heart. When our heart is aligned with His, He can lead us into the incredible. We're better able to love others, think clearly, and become a vessel for signs, wonders, and miracles.

How have you been going to others as a substitute for going directly to God?

_____

_____

_____

_____

_____

_____

_____

_____

_____

_____

_____

_____

_____

_____

_____

_____

_____

_____

_____

_____

_____

PRAY

Lord, You are more than enough for me.
Nothing is sweeter than Your presence. Discipline me
to seek You as opposed to settling for substitutes.
AMEN.

Rhythms of Grace

Are you tired? Worn out? Burned out on religion?
Come to Me. Get away with Me and you'll recover your life.
I'll show you how to take a real rest. Walk with Me and work with
Me—watch how I do it. Learn the unforced rhythms of grace. I won't
lay anything heavy or ill-fitting on you. Keep company with Me and
you'll learn to live freely and lightly.
—MATTHEW 11:28–30 THE MESSAGE

Rest is more than a vacation, a long-overdue nap, or a trip to the spa. Self-care is important to recharge our mind, body, and spirit. But you can do all these things and still feel emotionally and spiritually exhausted. *REST* stands for (R)eleasing (E)very (S)abotaging (T)hought. It is our thoughts that hijack our peace and pollute our minds with worry. The Word says to learn the *unforced* rhythms of grace. If God is inviting us to learn it, that means it doesn't come naturally. We can begin by reflecting upon the thoughts we're thinking when we start to feel anxious. This is how we take our thoughts captive and make them obedient to Christ as directed in II Corinthians 10:5. We cannot defeat toxic thoughts if we're unaware that they're in the driver's seat. As we release the need for perfection, continuous creation, and hustle, we begin to enter the rhythm of grace—a more peaceful and productive pace. When we're focusing and fixing, we're operating from the soil of lack, which yields the empty fruit of weariness, overwhelm, and distrust. But when we operate from the soil of possibility, watered by supernatural trust and blessed thinking, we get to joyously experience more than we can fathom.

What thoughts are creating anxiety as opposed to a peaceful flow?

_____
_____
_____
_____
_____
_____
_____
_____
_____
_____
_____
_____
_____
_____
_____
_____
_____

PRAY

God, help me to learn how to truly REST
in You as a lifestyle, not a vacation.
You are an excursion I never want to leave.
And because of Jesus, I don't have to.

AMEN.

Greater Indwelling

Peace I leave with you; My peace I give you.
I do not give to you as the world gives.
Do not let your hearts be troubled and do not be afraid.
—JOHN 14:27 NIV

As Jesus neared the end of His earthly ministry, He essentially explains to the disciples that the best thing that could happen was for Him to leave. With His departure would come a supernatural deposit that would fulfill the Scriptures and feed manna to the masses for generations to come. Jesus was talking about the Holy Spirit. No longer would it be something they would only see when Jesus performed a miracle, taught a sermon, or walked on water. No longer would God's voice only be clear to the prophets. Instead, His followers would personally experience the indwelling of the Holy Spirit inside their mind and being. Jesus also refers to the Holy Spirit as "My peace." Perhaps now we can understand how Jesus was able to calm the storms, be unmoved by demons, and bless those who betrayed and cursed Him. The indwelling of the Holy Spirit, and the peace that comes with it, is what God desires most for us. It makes obedience natural. It makes trusting God through the impossible normal. And it allows us to experience limitless living the way God always intended. We don't have to wait for the Spirit to fall *on* us, when God has permitted the Spirit to reside *within* us. When Jesus left, He was really making room for the Holy Spirit to flow in the lives of the disciples—and specifically in your life too.

What needs to leave your life in order for you to make room for a greater indwelling of the Holy Spirit?

PRAY

Lord, clear the clutter clogging my heart and mind.
Make me a tabernacle for Your Spirit
and a sanctuary for Your Presence.
AMEN.

Every Prayer Counts

All those the Father gives Me will come to Me,
and whoever comes to Me I will never drive away.
—JOHN 6:37 NIV

Perfectionism pollutes our perception of our time with God. The enemy loves to twist our view of our quiet time with God, putting it on trial and accusing us of not being "good enough." As a result, we pick ourselves apart...evaluating our prayer performance...criticizing ourselves for having wandering thoughts or less than impressive prayers....We judge the amount of time we spent, how we felt, and our inability to feel the presence of God. Ultimately, we put our spiritual intimacy on trial in the recesses of our minds. Our beliefs about our worthiness and readiness slowly become wounded with worry and infected with a deadly strand of self-doubt. The worst is when we doubt and judge our standing with the Father. But God says no more! He never looks down upon us, and He doesn't grade us on our prayers! With God, nothing is wasted—no moment of thanksgiving, no moment of praise. No moment of worship or communication with God is insignificant, not even a simple "Hello," "Thank You," or "I love You." When God calls us to deeper and higher levels of communion, he does *not* use condemnation. He uses invitation and affirmation. God wants us to see us as He sees us, which is wanted and wonderful. Moments of stillness and fellowship give us a truer picture of ourselves. God will never drive you away. As He makes clear in Jeremiah 31:3 NIV, "I have loved you with an everlasting love; I have drawn you with unfailing kindness." He wants you to come as you are and to come constantly. It's His favorite part of being your Father.

How have you been judgmental of your prayer time with God?

Lord, I thank You that every prayer I pray is heard.
Further my desire for deep communion with You.

AMEN.

Kingdom-Seeking

But seek ye first the kingdom of God, and His righteousness;
and all these things shall be added unto you.
—MATTHEW 6:33 KJV

Blessing is an inside job. Before we can bless others, we must become a house where blessing is capable of flowing. Desire requires development before it becomes a reality. The fullness of God's presence and plan is missing in far too many lives because we are unwilling to be rebuilt. God is Creator. Jesus is Resurrector. The Holy Spirit is Counselor. In Him, we have the divine ability to create, resurrect (bring back to life), and be a catalyst for hope, direction, and clarity in the lives of others. However, that good work must happen *in* us before it manifests *through* us. It starts with being surrendered to a divine building process…not a moment…not a quick encounter. A process that enables God's promises to take root in us. It is then that we are able to flow. That life, light, salt, and fire then comes out of us effortlessly. What is in you is what comes out. God isn't trying to get you to *do* more; God is seeking to get more of Himself—His heart, His mind, and His ability—in you. A supernatural infilling requires intentional stillness. Imagine trying to fill a cup when it's moving all over the place. God doesn't ask us to be still in order to sideline us but to refresh us and supply all our needs. In order for miracles to manifest, we must first become a place, an internal incubator, where miracles are capable of happening. Miracles can't happen if we're too busy to kneel before God and bathe in His presence. Seeking the kingdom by creating time and space for solitude and communion with God is how God shapes us and supplies us for the "more" He has in store for us.

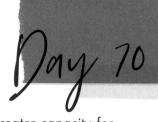

How is God seeking to use stillness to create in you a greater capacity for your calling?

_____

_____

_____

_____

_____

_____

_____

_____

_____

_____

_____

_____

_____

_____

_____

_____

_____

_____

_____

PRAY

God, create in me a capacity for miracles.
As I seek You persistently, build me from the inside out
so that I can be the blessing You built me to be.

AMEN.

The Path to Greater

Blessed is she who believes that
what the Lord has promised will be fulfilled.
—LUKE 1:45

We often get excited at the thought of a new blessing on the way. We wanna name it, frame it, and claim it. But that's not God's formula. God says, "Blessed is she who has believed." Belief precedes the blessing. In fact, it invites it. Better yet, belief *unleashes* it. We see in Luke 1:45 that God isn't talking about sending a blessing; He is outlining His strategy for our accessibility. God wants us to *BE* blessed, not just *GET* blessed things. Why? We're not here for the purpose of receiving. We're here to manifest—to unleash what's already within! If we are blessed, that means we carry the blessing...and we attract blessing too! That's what God is after. He wants everything about you to operate in the blessing frequency so that you can *BE* a bigger blessing. Belief is the bridge to greater blessing.

How has this elevated your thinking about what it means to "be blessed" versus "getting" a blessing?

_____

_____

_____

_____

_____

_____

_____

_____

_____

_____

_____

_____

_____

_____

_____

_____

PRAY

Lord, forgive me for praying for "stuff."
Elevate my thinking and my understanding of how You operate.
Bless my mind, make me unafraid of what You've deposited
within me, and anchor me in a posture of service.

AMEN.

Walking in God's Footsteps

"The soldiers took sheep and cattle from the plunder,
the best of what was devoted to God, in order to sacrifice them
to the LORD your God at Gilgal." But Samuel replied:
"Does the LORD delight in burnt offerings and sacrifices as much as in
obeying the LORD? To obey is better than sacrifice,
and to heed is better than the fat of rams."
—I SAMUEL 15:21–22 NIV

As I delve into the Old Testament, I see so vividly one theme woven into the fabric of each and every spiritual journey. God just wants us to trust Him. Obedience isn't a heavy thing; it's a holy thing. It's purely about alignment, not perfection, sacrifice, or achievement. In this season, I believe God is inviting you to hear His voice, to believe His promises (yes, the ones that seem to be collecting dust), and to follow what He says and shows…not because He owns us but because He loves us. We're not disobedient because we're bad. It's because, in some way, our trust in God is broken. We prefer our way because it's familiar. To step into the future God has for you, your faith must align with God's footsteps. Obedience is more blessed, more powerful, and more necessary than sacrifice.

How do you define obedience? Is the thought of it heavy? Scary? Why?

_____
_____
_____
_____
_____
_____
_____
_____
_____
_____
_____
_____
_____
_____
_____
_____
_____
_____

PRAY

Lord, I know my best is found in obedience.
You have perfect vision, plans, and timing. Help me to trust
how much You love me so that I can trust and act upon
any and everything You ask of me. Mature my heart to match
Your motivations. In Your Most Holy Name,

AMEN.

Surrendered Steps

For the source of your pleasure
is not in my performance
or the sacrifices I might offer to you.
—PSALM 51:17 TPT

So often we think that God's blessings are going to come faster if we're busy and doing all we can to make things happen on our end. Not so. God doesn't need our help. God needs our heart. All our actions should be out of the overflow of a love relationship with Christ and a desire to move in step with His will, His heartbeat, and His direction. That's the essence of blessed obedience. It's not about proving, performing, or earning. Walking in obedience is more about alignment and a statement of trust in the everlasting goodness of God—and a desire to be where and what He needs as chosen vessels here to make manifest His glory. Obedience isn't supposed to be this ominous, heavy thing. It's an invitation to enter a faith adventure with God. The sacrifice God requires is not in what you do; it is found in the condition of a surrendered heart.

How have you been trying to "help" God answer your prayers?

_____

_____

_____

_____

_____

_____

_____

_____

_____

_____

_____

_____

_____

_____

_____

_____

PRAY

Lord, I surrender my ambition for Your agenda.
Subdue my anxiousness and give me a steadfast heart
that reflects a deep trust in You.

AMEN.

Blessing of Provision

The Lord will guarantee a blessing
on everything you do and
will fill your storehouses with grain.
The Lord Your God will bless you
in the land He is giving you.
—DEUTERONOMY 28:8 NLT

How sweet it is to know that God is guaranteed to bless you. It's exciting and reassuring. But we can often forget that some blessings are byproducts of alignment and obedience. The passage above makes clear that the blessing of provision isn't random. The blessing referenced is specifically and strategically attached to the land, the territory, and the assignment God is leading them into. God doesn't promise to bless us where we don't belong. How else would He usher us into our promised land? For this reason, blessing and obedience go hand in hand. It's not that we are striving to earn a blessing; that doesn't work. Instead, we are seeking to align with where God's presence, plan, path, and provision are already flowing. Far too many of our choices are *decided* but not truly *directed*. When you default to doing what you want, when you want, and how you want, God will let you. But it doesn't mean that the blessing of His provision and protection will be on upon your decision. It is, however, guaranteed to be upon His direction. It's time to stop trespassing in the land of our desires and to step into the territory of divine destiny.

Are you living in the land of your own decisions right now or in God's direction?

_____

_____

_____

_____

_____

_____

_____

_____

_____

_____

_____

_____

_____

_____

_____

_____

_____

PRAY

Lord, I trade my desires for Your direction.
Take me into the territory You have already prepared
for me to steward, amplify, and enjoy.

AMEN.

Spiritual Discipline

*By faith Noah, being warned of God
of things not seen as yet, moved with fear,
prepared an ark to the saving of his house;
by the which he condemned the world,
and became heir of the righteousness which is by faith.*
—HEBREWS 11:7 KJV

Noah was as patient as He was obedient. It was what protected him and preserved his legacy and his family. Patience showed because he took time to build the ark. After the flood, he sent a dove to test the land to see if it was firm enough for those on the ark to step out. Just because the storm was over, it didn't necessarily mean that God was ready to release them to step into a new territory. (The same goes for us after our storms.) How difficult it must have been to be trapped on that ark with all the animals and also his family, who was likely constantly asking, "Can we get off this thing and go outside now?" It takes a great deal of spiritual discipline to be able to make uncomfortable and unpopular decisions that no one else understands— especially when things appear to be just fine. Noah shows us that obedience is really a byproduct of spiritual intimacy—spending time with God and listening for His voice. Noah waited for a clear sign that it was time to emerge. God will give you clear signs too. Obedience is a unique mixture of patience and pursuit. Don't be moved by pressure or your own time line. But don't delay either. When God makes the land ready for your footsteps, own the moment.

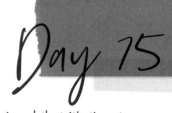

What "branches" has God been sending your way to signal that it's time to emerge from what you've built and enter your new territory?

Lord, let my belief always be evidenced
by my willingness to build accordingly to Your blueprint...
and to go when and where You lead.

AMEN.

God's Directive

For if you remain silent at this time, relief and deliverance
for the Jews will arise from another place, but you and
your father's family will perish. And who knows but that you
have come to your royal position for such a time as this?
—ESTHER 4:14 NIV

Unfavorable life circumstances often invite God's unbeatable blessing and favor. Take Esther. She was an orphan and a foreigner who found refuge and a life for herself by disguising her ethnicity and blending into the king's harem. She was basically in the palace's beauty school—drenched in the rules of her time and learning what a lady should do and be to please the powers that be. However, while she climbed the ranks, her people were being slaughtered. It was genocide. They had no advocate. For Esther to enter into the king's court without being summoned was an offense punishable by death. So when God called Esther to step up and speak up, to plead to the king on behalf of the Jewish people, God was asking her to do the unthinkable—to voluntarily blow her cover in a society that was killing her kind. But she was afraid to be herself. Hiding her true identity had been key to her survival. She came up with every excuse justifying why circumstances aren't right for her to do such a dangerous thing—to use her voice. It was not what women in her position were *supposed* to do. Esther was not incorrect, but she was not right either. It was true that the law forbade women from entering the king's court. But she was wrong about the law being more important than God's directive. In the end, she used her voice, saved her people, *and* became queen.

How have unfavorable circumstances been blocking you from operating in obedience?

_____

_____

_____

_____

_____

_____

_____

_____

_____

_____

_____

_____

_____

_____

_____

_____

_____

PRAY

Lord, You make a way out of no way.
You've already planned a pathway through the valley of
impossibility. Help me to operate with faith, not just facts.
AMEN.

Danger Zones

When you walk, your steps will not be hampered;
when you run, you will not stumble.
—PROVERBS 4:12 NIV

God's divine invitations are intentionally inconvenient. He sends us to unpopular places to prepare us before He enlarges our territory. The method may appear risky, and it will most certainly challenge what we think about ourselves, our beauty, our readiness, and our ability. However, the uncomfortableness that comes with a calling will reveal which broken beliefs are blocking our entry into bigger. God will do what it takes to capture our heart and correct our vision. And the divine invitation to lead anew will challenge our hidden attachment to our circumstances, our conformity, and our comfort zone.

The call to lead will ultimately reveal what and in whom we really trust. Do we trust *what* we know, or do we trust *who* we know? Divine leadership, which is the mantle of every woman, requires a willingness to surrender control and actively align with God's leading…especially when it doesn't make sense. Obedience tests our trust, unmasks hidden idols, and reveals true fears. The danger zone is not where we are going. The real danger is where we are staying. That's why God uses radical methods to disrupt us and redirect us. He loves us too much to leave us. As we walk in obedience, we'll walk through the doorways of destiny.

In what ways is God asking you to do something that seems risky or unpopular?

_____

_____

_____

_____

_____

_____

_____

_____

_____

_____

_____

_____

_____

_____

_____

_____

_____

_____

PRAY

*Lord, no circumstance is too dangerous for You
to achieve victory. Thank You for making me
a dangerous woman designed to win and not stumble.*

AMEN.

Going Where God Guides

Now the Lord is that Spirit:
and where the Spirit of the Lord is, there is liberty.
—II CORINTHIANS 3:17 KJV

In many areas of life, we have to ask for permission before we can walk through a new doorway, climb the career ladder, or even do what we love. Obeying man-made rules is not always a bad thing. They are often a blessed thing that give our lives structure, maturity, and discipline. But there are also times that man-made traditions and conventions conflict with where God is guiding. Never forget that the most blessed lane you can live in is wherever the Holy Spirit flows. Scripture reminds us that liberty resides where the Spirit of the Lord is. Liberty means freedom, authority, favor, ability, prepared soil, abundance, healing, joy, anointing, limitless possibility, and a place of permission. That is just an inkling of who God is. The Holy Spirit is where the blessing—the provision, protection and promise—is waiting. The "it" you've been praying, waiting, and looking for is found in the center of God's presence. And it's where we always want to be. Remember also that you carry the Holy Spirit inside. So going where God guides isn't necessarily about working harder; it can also be about trusting deeper. Or encouraging someone. Giving. Forgiving. Or simply resting. Allowing the Spirit of the Lord to rule and reign in your heart and mind ensures that you arrive at your intended destination.

Day 78

Where do you need to give yourself permission to ditch protocol or trade it for unpredictable possibility?

PRAY

Lord, I long to live in the lane You have paved for me.
Drench me in Your Holy Spirit as I walk unapologetically
in Your gifts and assignment.

AMEN.

Zone of Obedience

But the Lord said to me, "Do not say, 'I am too young.'
You must go to everyone I send you to and say whatever
I command you. Do not be afraid of them, for I am with you
and will rescue you," declares the Lord.
—JEREMIAH 1:7–8 NIV

The tug of a higher calling often invites us to use our voice and step into our next-level assignment. It also exposes our inner fears and insecurities. That's how we know it's our calling—the comfort zone keeps 'em covered up. The glory zone brings all the "stinking thinking" to the surface. Take Jeremiah. In Jeremiah 1, God calls Jeremiah to use his voice and deliver a prophecy that warns the people of calamity on the horizon. Jeremiah immediately explains to God that he is "just a child"—too young and not ready for such a task. God shuts that down quickly, essentially saying, "Don't tell Me what you're not capable of. I reside in you. I made you. If all things are possible with Me, then with Me living in you, there is nothing we can't do." We must remember that things are not always as they appear...especially when it comes to the way God works. We must "stop judging by mere appearances" (John 7:24 NIV). Faith is communicated on a higher frequency—one that requires spiritual eyes to see the way the Spirit of God moves. Further, God can never, ever be confined by a world He created. There are no rules on earth that God is bound by. Seeing with spiritual eyes in a physical world is the essence of spiritual maturity and the key to operating in the zone of obedience that takes us into blessed opportunity and overflow.

How is God showing that you are indeed ready to step into your next-level mission?

*Lord, continue to mature me in the zone of obedience.
Remove anything in me that stands in the way of me
following Your will and way.*

AMEN.

Bridge Being

The Lord had said to Abram, "Go from your country,
your people and your father's household
to the land I will show you."
—GENESIS 12:1 NIV

We've been taught to grow where we're planted but not how to go when directed. We're warned not to mess up, so we overthink and, in many ways, over-pray—Meaning that we sometimes use prayer as a way to avoid taking action. We don't know how to uproot ourselves (to shift) when it's time to replant; that's why we can feel stuck. Being still, even waiting on the Lord, when God has already said "Go" isn't obedience; it's fear. Or stubbornness. We don't always know where to begin when it comes to entering something new. And we certainly don't learn how to truly lead other people. However, you are a unique expression of an idea of God meant to lead others into more of God's goodness. If God meant for us to stay in one place, He would have given us roots as opposed to feet. We're not here to hide. Hiding surpasses the sacred. Your life is a one-of-a-kind bridge to God and His game plan. You deny others entry and passage when you live out of alignment...when you pretend...and when you procrastinate. But when you step into your anointing—and when you allow God to manifest whatever He wants, regardless of traditional or archaic mindsets—you end up connecting others to the piece of God that's long been missing in their lives. When you show up the way God made you and go wherever He sends you, people get a greater glimpse of your Manufacturer. It draws them closer to God, which is what He's after. Glory. Relationship. Intimacy. We don't get to script it; we can only surrender to it.

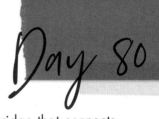

How do you desire your life to serve as a one-of-a-kind bridge that connects others to God's game plan?

_____

_____

_____

_____

_____

_____

_____

_____

_____

_____

_____

_____

_____

_____

_____

_____

_____

_____

_____

PRAY

Lord, thank You for equipping me to lead.
Upgrade my thinking so that it aligns with Your vision
for change and massive awakening.

AMEN.

Embracing Your Relevance

"Can a mother forget the baby at her breast and have no compassion on the child she has borne? Though she may forget, I will not forget you! See, I have engraved you on the palms of My hands; your walls are ever before Me."
—ISAIAH 49:15–16 NIV

Whether you've been following God for a day or a lifetime, we all have moments where we doubt we're on God's radar. Seasons of silence, or seasons where we've been negligent in pursuing His presence, can make us feel like we're forgotten. But we're not. It's not possible. The passage above confirms that we are etched into the very fiber of who God is. We can never be off the radar of God. He is concerned, practically obsessed, with every single thing that concerns you. At the end of the verse, it says, "your walls are ever before me." That's referring to your work, your desires, your affairs—everything that has to do with you…it's what your life is building. God is the Architect. Your face and the essence of who you are matter so much to God that He engraved you on His hands. He doesn't go a moment without thinking of you, providing for you, and guarding and guiding you. Remember, a tattoo is permanent! It's also a choice. It's something carefully considered—an image you desire to have with you for a lifetime. That's how much God loves you. He chose you. Your life is forever in God's hands!

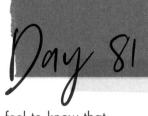

In what ways have you felt forgotten by God? How does it feel to know that God has engraved you on His hands?

Lord, I'm never forgotten. Everything that concerns me matters to You. May I live boldly in knowing that my future is secure with You.

AMEN.

Living Chosen

But you are a chosen race, a royal priesthood,
a holy nation, a people for his own possession,
that you may proclaim the excellencies of him
who called you out of darkness into his marvelous light.
—I PETER 2:9 ESV

In the midst of chaos, it can feel as though you're struggling to get on God's radar. But the truth is, you're chosen. God has always covered and protected you. You are loved and are being led for this very moment. Deep inside you sense it. There is more that God has for you. He has been trying to get to you—not just to rescue you but to speak to you, to comfort and replenish you. The obstacles of the past have been training you for something greater and higher. But never mistake a mess or moments of misery for abandonment. God has always had your back. What God has taken you through is all about what God is taking you to. You're here for a specific and special reason. You are incredibly important to God, and all of heaven is rooting for you. It's time to disrupt the inner narrative that tells you anything different. Your presence is needed as never before.

What does it mean and what would it look like for you to "live chosen"?

_____

_____

_____

_____

_____

_____

_____

_____

_____

_____

_____

_____

_____

_____

_____

_____

_____

_____

_____

_____

PRAY

Lord, my standing with You is intimate and incredible.
I am necessary because You said so, and I will live
in alignment with my divine birthright.

AMEN.

The Gifts of Fear

For God will never give you the spirit of fear,
but the Holy Spirit who gives you mighty power,
love, and self-control.
—II TIMOTHY 1:7 TPT

You're a target of the enemy because you're a threat to the enemy. The enemy is threatened by your awareness of your spiritual DNA and your owning your magnificence. To get us to doubt ourselves, the enemy pollutes our thoughts with a devious inner critic I refer to as *little me*. It's the voice of fear that hijacks our inner confidence by whispering doubt, worry, and hesitation. Think of *little me* as a bully who thrives on being our biggest insecurity. *Little me* is a master at invading our heart and hijacking our mind with disbelief. The sole mission and objective is to keep us from becoming all that we are meant to become. *Little me* is a straight-up hater, a voice that grows stronger and more persuasive each time we choose less instead of more. And *little me* needs and breathes fear like you and I need and breathe air. *Little me* is shrewd and slick, unapologetically brutal, and, at times, disguises itself as logic and rationale. Oh, and *little me* loves to keep us busy, with the mind swimming in a sea of self-sabotage and confusion. *Little me* will say whatever it takes to get you to shrink, settle, or waffle until you're eventually stagnant, self-conscious, stumbling, and stuck. Why? *Little me* knows that divine, God-glorifying momentum happens in our lives when we allow heaven to string together a series of bigger moments—moments where we believe bigger, decide bigger, and live bolder. God does not give us the spirit of fear, and that means you don't need to accept it. The only reason the spirit of fear hunts you down and taunts you with false illusions of difficulty, insecurity, and despair is because the enemy knows how great you really are.

How has your inner *little me* been tricking you out of living fully in faith and boldness?

_____

_____

_____

_____

_____

_____

_____

_____

_____

_____

_____

_____

_____

_____

_____

_____

PRAY

Lord, I refuse to live as a prisoner to fear
when I am really a warrior endowed with Your Holy Spirit,
mighty power, love, and incredible mind.
Direct my thoughts accordingly.
AMEN.

Simply Beautiful

You are altogether beautiful, my darling;
there is no flaw in you.
—SONG OF SONGS 4:7 NIV

Every woman longs to be seen, selected, and significant. Because the enemy knows this to be our deepest desire and therefore our greatest vulnerability, he uses self-doubt to contaminate it. This is especially true when you start dreaming and thinking about something beyond your current circumstances. *Little me* knows our insecurities...all of them. But *little me* also knows that our brilliance is our real beauty—that light-bearing part of us that shines so brightly that *little me* can't survive it. Remember, you're a target of the enemy because you're a threat to the enemy. The enemy diverts us from our destiny by putting dents in our confidence and chipping away at our self-image. So while beauty, however you define it, is what every woman desires, becoming it is also her greatest fear. The journey to purpose and unshakable, God-intended self-worth is ultimately about embracing our core essence, which is beauty. Beautifulness is what we crave—not because we need it, lost it, or must attain it as the world says but because it is who we already are. It is written: "You are altogether beautiful." *Altogether* means everything about you—all the flaws and the fantastic parts—working together to craft your uniqueness and supernatural significance. This isn't about being pretty. This is about owning your power, purpose, and path. It's time.

Day 84

What does it mean to own your beauty as your birthright?

PRAY

*Lord, You have already placed the fullness of Your beauty
in my DNA. Release my brilliance like never before.
Make me a threat to the enemy that brings You unlimited glory.*

AMEN.

Advancing the Kingdom

Don't hide your light! Let it shine for all;
let your good deeds glow for all to see,
so that they will praise your heavenly Father.
—MATTHEW 5:15–16 TLB

We aren't merely here to find our purpose; we are here to advance God's kingdom. That's our shared calling, master purpose, and ultimate assignment. It isn't finding your passion...or being a success story...but being a light that points others toward the Lord in all we do. For that reason, God wants you to succeed and to have visibility. God loves glory. He wants others to see Him in us so that out of the observance of how we live our lives, others would see Him. For that reason, our purpose isn't about us. It's not about our gifts, talent, passion, or anointing. Those are just tools that equip us to shine and reflect His goodness. Real significance isn't about you, what you want, how you're majestically built, or what you love. It's ultimately about God. Our purpose is to advance and showcase God's presence, to be a witness to His power. We are created by design to specifically glorify God. Our purpose and life's mission, then, is more about surrender and service than success. But, to be clear, God loves success too. It is just another pathway that heaven will use to invite more people into God's presence. How wonderful that God would recruit and design you as an essential part of His eternal plan.

Instead of asking what God wants, how can you find greater significance in asking *where* God needs you?

_____

_____

_____

_____

_____

_____

_____

_____

_____

_____

_____

_____

_____

_____

_____

_____

_____

PRAY

Lord, use me to expand the world's perception of You.
You are limitless, and I make myself available to be used
as Your ambassador in circles large and small. Send me.

AMEN.

Welcome Support

Wisdom is sweet to your soul.
If you find it, you will have a bright future,
and your hopes will not be cut short.
—PROVERBS 24:14 NLT

A key part of embracing our own significance is welcoming support. After all, God uses others to bless us, teach us, and mature us for our "now" and our "next." Look at the disciples—they needed Jesus to be more than their Messiah. They needed Him to be their teacher, comforter, and encourager. But it was Jesus's intention that they would receive the gift of His presence too. He wanted them to *become* the gifts and containers of His presence and wisdom so that others could grow. The same holds true with you. God desires that you live in communion with other people who can pour into you. But first you have to believe you're worthy. That was the real question the disciples had to ask themselves when Jesus invited them to leave all they had to follow Him. I imagine they had already been praying for a life shift...so they would experience something *more*. What will you do when the opportunity to shift shows up? Your shift will likely happen through encounters with other people who can teach, encourage, and build you up. But you must have eyes to see, a heart to receive, and a deep appreciation for wisdom. A new level of wisdom is an important key to unlocking the future that God has waiting for you. Be someone whom others want to pour into. Own your significance by operating with discipline and diligence. You're worthy of the wonderful. Believe it to receive it.

Why are you worthy of the wonderful?

Lord, You have already called me worthy and wonderful.
Surround me with extraordinary wisdom so that
I may grow into all You predestined for my life.

AMEN.

A New Creation

He who was seated on the throne said,
"I am making everything new!"
Then He said, "Write this down,
for these words are trustworthy and true."
—REVELATION 21:5 NIV

Too often, who we *decide* to be blocks us from who we were *born* to be. God loves us too much to leave us or lose us, so instead He splits us so that true significance can flow from within us. The method can feel messy, but the process is still part of a divine masterpiece. Sometimes God shakes up our lives and splits us open for something new to emerge. Finding significance isn't about reaching a new goal; it's about becoming a new creation. God will go to drastic lengths to get the attention of His daughters—and that most certainly includes you. You will no doubt experience drama and trauma that won't always make sense. But without pain, we'd never experience the refreshing gift of healing. The reason for heartbreak, betrayal, and loss may never be explained. If we desire a God-led life, we must get comfortable with mystery. Instead of seeking answers, we must seek first the kingdom of heaven—thirsting for God's heart, not just His hands. God knows what He's doing, and He doesn't owe us any explanations. When we've veered too deeply onto the wrong path, God will split us from ourselves and from whatever no longer serves as the bigger life waiting to emerge. Rest assured that adversity is a sign of your significance and a catalyst to awaken your next-level calling.

How is adversity actually a sign of your significance and a clue as to who you really are in God's eyes?

_____

_____

_____

_____

_____

_____

_____

_____

_____

_____

_____

_____

_____

_____

_____

_____

_____

_____

PRAY

Lord, awaken my next-level calling by aligning me
with my true identity. You have my attention.
Speak, for Your servant is listening.

AMEN.

Embrace Your Favor

But the angel reassured her, saying, "Do not yield to your fear,
Mary, for the Lord has found delight in you
and has chosen to surprise you with a wonderful gift.
—LUKE 1:30 TPT

Seemingly out of nowhere, God sends the angel Gabriel to visit a young girl named Mary. She is a virgin and engaged to wed a young man named Joseph. Gabriel greets Mary, saying, "Good morning! You're beautiful with God's beauty, beautiful inside and out! God [is] with you" (Luke 1:28 THE MESSAGE). This frightens Mary. Maybe it was seeing a genuine angel, or maybe it was his message—or all of the above. However, Gabriel tells Mary that she has nothing to fear and that she will become pregnant and give birth to a son named Jesus (vv. 30–31). Mary then asks a very legitimate question: "But how? I've never slept with a man" (v. 34). Gabriel explains that the Holy Spirit will come upon her (v. 35). Hmph! What an invitation to believe bigger, indeed! In this moment, disruption greets Mary with her greatest fear—not a fear of doing but the fear of being enough. Some translations use the word "favored" as opposed to "beautiful inside and out," but it's the beauty translation that speaks to significance. We each struggle to believe that we're divinely beautiful...not because of anything we've done or how we look but just because of who we are. That day, Gabriel invited Mary to believe beyond her biggest fear. She asked the same questions you and I do: Am I good enough? Am I beautiful? Am I favored, chosen by, and loved by God? I believe Mary had been wrestling with questioning her beauty and worth for some time. Gabriel was an unexpected answer—a "yes" straight from heaven that frightened her before it focused her.

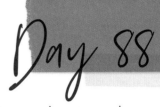

How has God been speaking to you about your significance, beauty, and favor?

_____

_____

_____

_____

_____

_____

_____

_____

_____

_____

_____

_____

_____

_____

_____

_____

_____

_____

_____

PRAY

Lord, You've chosen me to birth the incredible.
I accept the gift of Your favor for Your glory.
AMEN.

Unashamed Acceptance

God selected the common and the castoff,
whatever lacks status, so He could invalidate
the claims of those who think those things are significant.
—I CORINTHIANS 1:28 (THE VOICE)

Whether we are stay-at-home mothers, career women, in school, dealing with illness, recovering from divorce, or just trying to find our confidence…something causes all of us to ask the question, "Will God actually use me? Given my circumstances…given how things look or appear…and given who I've been and how others perceive and rely upon me, could God actually reinvent and use me for something glorious and new?" Self-doubt has a clear mission, which is to prevent you from stepping boldly into *your* mission. It wants to shrink your borders, bury your brilliance, and cripple the courage needed to be a living ripple-effector on the earth. Destiny is a call to boldness. Service to the King and kingdom-building happens when we embrace boldness and commit to building up others. That's true leadership. So here's the deal: saying yes to your higher purpose isn't going to be easy. Anything worth having is worth believing in. And believing in God isn't enough if you don't believe that, in Him, you're more than enough too. The key is to remember this: an unashamed woman is an unstoppable woman. God will use you in a greater way when you stop being ashamed of your calling. It's time to release your timidity and regrets and trade them in for resolve and readiness.

Where do you feel God guiding you to lead next?

PRAY

Lord, You've built me for bold adventures.
Help me not to waste time questioning my worth and readiness
and to instead maximize my God-given magnificence.

AMEN.

Brightly Lit Streets

The lives of good people are brightly lit streets.
—PROVERBS 13:9 THE MESSAGE

We often torment ourselves with questions about what we should and shouldn't do...who we should and shouldn't be...and where we do or don't belong. The truth is that anyplace God sends you is holy ground. So believe me when I say you matter, that your stories, ideas, dreams, gifts, and desires matter. Your adversity gives you depth. God needs people who have been through and overcome "stuff." Those are the messes that make a real message—one aligned in spirit and in truth. Your life and presence are a brightly lit street—but it's time to turn the lights on. It's time to be the voice, the gift-giver, and the creative force you are. It's time to speak up, step up, and stop hiding. I'm talking to your destiny—I'm intentionally speaking life into your future, because your future depends on it. And someone else's future depends on your mind shift, your boldness, and your "start" too. You don't need perfect conditions; you need surrender and a proactive willingness to let God use you in new and uncomfortable ways—now. Whether it's talking to a stranger on the street, connecting with a coworker, or sharing your journey (as small as it might seem) with a new or old friend, purpose unfolds from within us whenever we decide to be bold. Someone is waiting on you to come out of hiding. You matter more than you could ever know.

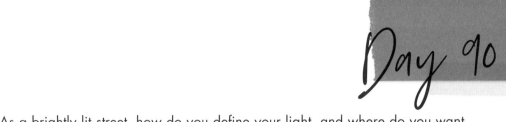

As a brightly lit street, how do you define your light, and where do you want it to lead others?

_____

_____

_____

_____

_____

_____

_____

_____

_____

_____

_____

_____

_____

_____

_____

_____

_____

PRAY

Lord, Your significance defines my own.
I am enough, ready, and worthy.
Illuminate my path as I shine brighter for Your glory.
AMEN.

Release the Old

Stop imitating the ideals and opinions of the culture around you,
but be inwardly transformed by the Holy Spirit
through a total reformation of how you think.
This will empower you to discern
God's will as you live a beautiful life,
satisfying and perfect in His eyes.
—ROMANS 12:2 TPT

Over time, conditioning can block calling and chip away at our courage. The pressure to do what we've always done, what we've always been taught, and what we've always seen can block us from discerning and entering the new God has for us. It becomes easy to miss the everyday, inconspicuous invitations from heaven to experience *more*. What we believe about ourselves and what we believe we're worthy to experience are often merely a regurgitation of what others have told us we should be or shouldn't do. But the living Word and will of God cannot be contained, and it is certainly not predictable. God is inviting you to release old patterns of thinking and truly adopt His mind. That means hearing His voice and operating from fresh revelation, not observation. It takes courage to renew one's mind and challenge outdated beliefs and paradigms. Know that your next-level mission and calling aren't found in the past. As you embrace God's new vision for you, you'll start seeing new pathways and doors open. A woman on purpose will supernaturally invite everything she needs to thrive.

How have you been limiting yourself with a "protocol mindset" (doing what others say) as opposed to a "permission mindset" (going where God guides)? Why?

_____

_____

_____

_____

_____

_____

_____

_____

_____

_____

_____

_____

_____

_____

PRAY

Lord, thank You for the wisdom that got me to this point.
I release what no longer belongs,
including old ways, habits, and thoughts.
My desire is to hear Your voice and live in revelation.

AMEN.

Develop Your Gifts

For to everyone who has will more be given,
and he will have an abundance. But from the one who has not,
even what he has will be taken away.
—MATTHEW 25:29 ESV

Talents often hide gifts. Initially, it can be tricky to tell our talents from our gifts, but distinguishing them can be life-changing. Our proficiencies—the things we're good at—can end up becoming our formed identity, reflecting the person we decided to become and the path we chose to take. As such, talents often mask purpose and, with it, our born identity. Gifts, on the other hand, are the things God uniquely prewired us to do—God-touched abilities that reflect an aspect of Him and help others too. Our talents are things we learned to do; gifts are the things we were born to do. And gifts are the attributes that God has specifically anointed to enable us to unlock destiny, healing, belief, and growth in others. Your best talents, the ones you've likely become known for, the things you're really good at, are like super-skills. You should be good at them; you've worked to become so. Anything you focus on has the ability to flourish. However, your gifts are your God-given superpowers. It takes courage to believe in yourself and develop your capacity to fulfill your calling. Others are praying for someone just like you to cross their path. It's time to develop your ability to take your superpowers to others' super problems.

Day 92

What attributes and abilities do you feel are your talents (super-skills you've learned to master) versus your gifts (superpowers you were born to provide)?

PRAY

Father, give me the courage to distinguish
what I can do from what I am called to do.
AMEN.

Own Your Gifts

*Each person is given something to do
that shows who God is.*
—I CORINTHIANS 12:7 THE MESSAGE

God was incredibly meticulous and thoughtful when it came to your divine design. Nothing about your life is an accident or a coincidence. To the contrary, everything about you is actually a clue as to what type of impact you are here to have. These clues are revealed through our individual gifts. Our gifts are guides that lead us into God's game plan. Gifts are the agents of purpose and the bedrock of calling. They exist to provide laser focus in your life by showing you what your life is really about. Your purpose isn't just to believe; it's to activate your belief in such a way that you impact, serve, and ignite others. By becoming more aware of and embracing your gifts, you're able to be more intentional with your time, talents, and energy. Jesus was a perfect example of focus. His gifts of healing, teaching, serving, and loving both fueled and focused His mission. It takes courage to narrow your focus and own your gifts. When you focus on your gifts (not just your abilities), your gifts focus you too.

What are your gifts, and how are they clues to what you're here to be and do?

_____

_____

_____

_____

_____

_____

_____

_____

_____

_____

_____

_____

_____

_____

_____

PRAY

*Lord, thank You for being specific with the gifts
and abilities You've given me. I'm honored and ready
to step into the next-level mission You have for my life.
Groom my gifts for Your glory.*

AMEN.

Activate Your Gifts

For if the willingness is there,
the gift is acceptable according to what one has,
not according to what one does not have.
—II CORINTHIANS 8:12 NIV

Gifts are what you've been given to give to others. We're here to teach, to serve, and to *gift out* what's been *gifted in* to us. The beautiful thing about your gifts is that they enable you to align with God's master plan and maximize your individual calling at the same time. This happens in three ways. First, your gifts enable you to fulfill God's will here on earth. He has placed the solutions, the refreshing, and the presence others are longing for inside *you*. You get to be an extension of His hands, feet, and heart by aligning your gifts with those assigned to you and in need of your uniqueness. Second, your gifts move others forward into their promised land, future, and destiny. When you help others with something that is difficult for them but easy for you, you serve a bridge that connects others to something greater, bigger, sweeter, and more blessed. Third, your gifts improve lives. This doesn't have to be monumental to be impactful and meaningful. It takes courage to lead in alignment with your gifting. Don't worry about what you don't have. God is going to bless what you do have beyond your wildest imagination. You're right where you're supposed to be for God's next big move. It's time to activate your gifts and lead others into the light along the way.

How do you desire to move others forward and improve the lives of those you have access to?

_____

_____

_____

_____

_____

_____

_____

_____

_____

_____

_____

_____

_____

_____

_____

_____

_____

PRAY

Lord, show me where I can have
a meaningful impact by using my gifts
in simple, unique, and everyday ways.
AMEN.

Expect More

And He did not do many miracles there
because of their lack of faith.
—MATTHEW 13:58 NIV

There is never a moment when God doesn't want you to expect the best. Bigger belief and high expectancy are a breeding ground for miracles. So whenever you're unsure about what God wants you to do, here it is: live boldly and unapologetically give yourself permission to believe without limits on every occasion. Expectancy goes to the heart of believing bigger and living bolder. However, to have an incredible impact, we must have an incredible self-image. You are indeed a weapon, beautiful but deadly and dangerous. God intends that we be a threat to the enemy by being a light that drives out the darkness. Believe in your beauty but also believe in your power. You were built to destroy the enemy. The enemy doesn't want you to see yourself as a destroyer. He wants us to live timidly and to see ourselves as victims, intrinsically vulnerable, as those being hunted and at risk of being taken. We have every reason to expect more. God is the king of "suddenly" and is always sending us what we need. God speaks in cans, not in can'ts. "God can do anything...far more than [we] could ever imagine or guess or request in [our] wildest dreams! He does it not by pushing us around but by working within us . . ." (Ephesians 3:20 THE MESSAGE). Expectancy takes courage—to press through disappointment and believe that destiny has a marvelous place just for you. Commit to having an optimistic and expectant attitude from within—to operate from a place of positive anticipation, not worry or hesitation.

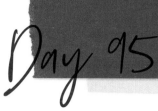

In what areas do you need to get your level of faith and expectancy way up?

Lord, nothing is impossible or too hard for You.
Help me to operate in my expectations,
not my experiences.

AMEN.

Start Before You're Ready

*Do not despise these small beginnings,
for the LORD rejoices to see the work begin....*
—ZECHARIAH 4:10 NLT

"If it is meant to be" is not a biblical principle—it's a hollow mantra that gives us permission to passively play with God as opposed to pursuing our assignment. The enemy wants you to stay in a place of waiting on the right time, delaying to become who you were meant to be. *Waiting* is one of those misleading words. According to Isaiah 40:31, "They that *wait* upon the LORD shall renew their strength" (KJV, emphasis mine). *Wait* is actually an action word. Other translations say *trust, hope,* and *look for Him.* What if "to wait" meant "to align"? To actively look for and step into holy flow? That would read, then, that they who align with the Lord shall renew their strength. The best athletes in the world get stronger, or renew their strength, in the off-season. Waiting is a time for preparation. Starting before you're ready is the ultimate faith step, and faith steps are the kind of steps that God not only orders but prioritizes. The circumstances will never be perfect. Just remember that perfectionism, getting ready to get ready, isn't a friend to your purpose. It's not only a barrier; it's poison. It takes courage to be a catalyst. But we have to give God something to work with. He can't bless steps that we never take, a dream we never deploy, and a mission we never start.

What is it God is asking you to start, reinvent, or take to the next level?

_____
_____
_____
_____
_____
_____
_____
_____
_____
_____
_____
_____
_____
_____
_____
_____
_____
_____
_____
_____

PRAY

Lord, detox me of procrastination and perfectionism.
With You, I have everything I need to begin and thrive.

AMEN.

Stop Auditioning

Fear of man is a dangerous trap,
but to trust in God means safety.
—PROVERBS 29:25 TLB

The less you care what others think, the more your life will expand. Not everyone will understand your dream or vision. They don't have to—it's not their vision. It's nice to have support, but you must be careful not to draw confidence from the approval of others. When we do that, we give them our keys. Someone else gets to sit in our sacred driver's seat. You don't need anyone's permission to be powerful, bold, or brilliant. And you don't need anyone's permission to share your voice, tell your story, or launch your dream. You only need God's blessing. Instead of waiting on others to validate your vision while you doubt your God-given desires, start doubting your doubts. It's the spirit of fear and overload of opinions from others that make us shrink and second-guess. God has no desire for you to put yourself in a people-pleasing, protocol-paved prison. God's spirit within you holds the key to unlocking your potential and creating miraculous life shifts. You're responsible for doing what God has placed in your heart. It takes courage to stop auditioning, striving, proving, and looking for validation. You're not man-made, you're God-made.

Whose opinion and approval do you need to release in order shift into your next level of destiny?

_____

_____

_____

_____

_____

_____

_____

_____

_____

_____

_____

_____

_____

_____

_____

_____

PRAY

*Lord, I thank You that I am made in Your image
and therefore more than enough. Give me
supernatural courage to live worthy and ready.*
AMEN.

Invest in You

*For where your treasure is,
there your heart will be also.*
—MATTHEW 6:21 NIV

Most believers invest in everything except their gifts and purpose. For some reason, we have adopted a dysfunctional belief that if it's a God-thing, then it's up to God to make the thing happen. That's not scriptural. Obedience and alignment always come with sacrifice and investment. It cost the disciples everything to walk with Christ. They made an investment to be mentored and taught for their spiritual growth. Investment is a sign of seriousness. It's not about money or an amount; it's about alignment—following God's voice and investing in His vision. We must be willing to invest in both the expansion gospel *and* a personal growth plan. The gospel can't grow if we don't. While God's qualification criteria for promotion is indeed different than society's, it's no reason to be lazy or take our anointing for granted. That's immature and makes us spiritually unbalanced and ineffective. We are to be good stewards of our time, treasure, and talents. A new blessing often comes through a new person with something new to teach you. Self-investment, pouring into your purpose and superpowers, is a powerful way to build divine confidence and to show God you're serious rather than just giving lip service. Faith without works is empty. So invest in what grows your ability to take action with wisdom. Development and process is so very important to God. It takes courage to be a woman who puts her money where her mission is.

What investments can you make to sow life into your dreams and prepare you for higher purpose?

Lord, make me an investor who values wisdom, strategy, and quality mentorship. I want to stay dressed and ready for Your service.

AMEN.

Finish What You Started

*So now finish doing it as well, so that your readiness in desiring it
may be matched by your completing it out of what you have.*
—II CORINTHIANS 8:11 ESV

When we finish what we've started and press through the doubt that
sprouts along the way, the enemy has nothing left to say. Nada. But we
have to put ideas and plans into practice. Inspiration without implementation is
a figment of our imagination. Finishing breeds supernatural confidence, and it
rebuilds the broken bridges of inner distrust that we've allowed to deteriorate
over the years. Much of fear is self-imposed. When we leave things lingering,
when we start this and that but never finish, we weaken the internal bridges
that connect us to us. Because we teach ourselves whether we can be trusted
to follow through on our own dreams and desires, we stop trusting ourselves
when we don't finish. But we were built to finish. We must watch out for the
assassins after our anointing—delay; its sister, perfectionism; and its cousin,
distraction. They are decoys sent to divert our attention, keep us occupied with
the unnecessary, and stop us from crossing over into our promised land. It
takes courage to be a woman who says yes to her calling and follows through
with it. All of heaven rejoices when we cross the finish line. Know that you're
capable and called to complete your mission for such a time as this.

What is it you've struggled to finish? What simple things can you do today to move you toward completion?

PRAY

Lord, help me to be a woman who finishes strong.

AMEN.

Step In

You have not passed this way before.
—JOSHUA 3:4 ESV

God is a God of impeccable order, intention, and structure. Nothing that has occurred in your life is a coincidence. Everything you've encountered—even the awful things—have been part of your journey. And while you might intrinsically know that you're on some kind of journey, you may not know exactly where you are, where you're going, or, most importantly, why you're ultimately here. That's okay. Becoming comfortable with mystery is one of the ways we grow our faith. God designed you for a powerful purpose, and you're already being guided by it. It's what led you to this moment. You're a messenger and a carrier of the Holy Spirit—the same power that conquered the grave. God didn't intend for us to simply read about miraculous encounters in a book thousands of years old. God intends that *we* be the book, the living Word—a living manifestation of God's unlimited abilities and promises. In Romans 9:17, God says, "I raised you up for this very purpose, that I might display My power in you and that My name might be proclaimed in all the earth" (NIV)! You're a masterpiece—and an essential component in God's master plan. It's time to ditch the distractions, own your anointing, and kick fear goodbye. This is your charge to step into your gifts, unleash your superpowers, and give credence to your dreams and desires. It's time to be you. That takes *real* courage. But unleashing the real you is exactly what God needs you to do. Know that if heaven has called you to it, it's God's job to see you through it.

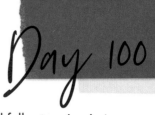

How will you commit to believing bigger, living bolder, and fully stepping in to what God has destined you to be and do?

_____

_____

_____

_____

_____

_____

_____

_____

_____

_____

_____

_____

_____

_____

_____

_____

_____

_____

_____

PRAY

Lord, have Your way in my life. Take me on an adventure that expands my capacity and leads others directly to You. I trust You.

AMEN.

Believing Bigger is the formula for miracle moments and movements in your life. We are *regularly* supposed to have unpredictable, spirit-unleashing encounters with others. Miracles—and moments oozing with purpose—are intended to be commonplace, not rare. We're supposed to change the atmosphere. But that can't happen if the daughters of heaven called to live as bold believers continue to become an endangered species. We can't continue to shrink and be held hostage by limiting self-belief.

It's time to come out of hiding. Deep within, you know there is an unlived life waiting—one with only your name on it, One God has destined you for all along. You may not be able to fully see it, but you can sense it. *Bigger* is indeed calling you.

Know that to unleash the greater you, God will disrupt and dismantle you. He will humble you. He will use any means necessary to rebuild you anew. But only because your life's mission is magnificent and you are indeed incredibly necessary.

Walk with courage as you unlearn who you have been and discover who you really are, what you possess, and how God designed you.

Fear is a liar, but it is also a guide leading you into God's game plan for your life. You are a target of the enemy because you are a threat to the enemy. But you are also covered by the God who is with you, who is coauthoring your future right now. When God says yes, there is not a devil in hell that can say no. Defy the status quo. Defy tradition. And defy gravity. Do what seems impossible, unthinkable, and untimely. Christ defied all the odds, and so should you! I know that the best is within you and that superpowers are indeed waiting to manifest through you. I believe in your beauty, boldness, and brilliance. You are a miracle in motion ready to start a movement.

My prayer is that you would dare to *believe bigger* in you too. You're ready.

Best blessings,

marghawn

MARSHAWN EVANS DANIELS is a reinvention strategist and life coach mentoring women around the world to live bolder in the areas of faith and business. As a serial entrepreneur, TV personality, creator of the Godfidence movement and founder of SHE Profits, she helps women turn ideas into income and faith into action. A former sports attorney, Miss America finalist, and competitor on *The Apprentice*, she left a high-powered law firm and turned her passion for people into a multimillion-dollar enterprise. Appearing regularly on CNN, Fox Business, and ESPN, her clients range from Rolls Royce, HP, Nike, Home Depot, and Ernst & Young to everyday dreamers seeking to find their voice and maximize their potential. Named Woman Entrepreneur of the Year by the Atlanta Business League, she is a graduate of Georgetown University Law Center and is admitted to practice before the Supreme Court. She is also a member of Alpha Kappa Alpha Sorority, a Harry S. Truman scholar, and a former US Ambassador to the International Summit of Achievement in Dublin, Ireland. Marshawn is passionate about purpose, futurist thinking, manifestation, entrepreneurship, motherhood, and traveling the globe with her husband Jack.

LIVE YOUR FAITH

Dear Friend,

This book was prayerfully crafted with you, the reader, in mind—every word, every sentence, every page—was thoughtfully written, designed, and packaged to encourage you...right where you are this very moment. At DaySpring, our vision is to see every person experience the life-changing message of God's love. So, as we worked through rough drafts, design changes, edits and details, we prayed for you to deeply experience His unfailing love, indescribable peace, and pure joy. It is our sincere hope that through these Truth-filled pages your heart will be blessed, knowing that God cares about you—your desires and disappointments, your challenges and dreams.

He knows. He cares. He loves you unconditionally.

BLESSINGS!
THE DAYSPRING BOOK TEAM

Additional copies of this book and
other DaySpring titles can be purchased
at fine retailers everywhere.
Order online at dayspring.com
or
by phone at 1-877-751-4347